The Observer's Pocket Series

BRITISH
STEAM LOCOMOTIVES

The Observer Books

A POCKET REFERENCE SERIES COVERING A
WIDE RANGE OF SUBJECTS

Natural History
BIRDS
BIRDS' EGGS
BUTTERFLIES
LARGER MOTHS
COMMON INSECTS
WILD ANIMALS
ZOO ANIMALS
WILD FLOWERS
GARDEN FLOWERS
FLOWERING TREES
  AND SHRUBS
HOUSE PLANTS
CACTI
TREES
GRASSES
COMMON FUNGI
LICHENS
POND LIFE
FRESHWATER FISHES
SEA FISHES
SEA AND SEASHORE
GEOLOGY
ASTRONOMY
WEATHER
CATS
DOGS
HORSES AND PONIES

Transport
AIRCRAFT
AUTOMOBILES
COMMERCIAL VEHICLES
SHIPS
MANNED SPACEFLIGHT
UNMANNED
  SPACEFLIGHT
BRITISH STEAM
  LOCOMOTIVES

The Arts etc
ARCHITECTURE
CATHEDRALS
CHURCHES
HERALDRY
FLAGS
PAINTING
MODERN ART
SCULPTURE
FURNITURE
MUSIC
POSTAGE STAMPS
POTTERY & PORCELAIN
BRITISH
  AWARDS & MEDALS

Sport
ASSOCIATION FOOTBALL
CRICKET

Cities
LONDON

The Observer's Book of

BRITISH STEAM LOCOMOTIVES

H. C. CASSERLEY

WITH OVER 140
BLACK AND WHITE ILLUSTRATIONS

FREDERICK WARNE & CO LTD
FREDERICK WARNE & CO INC
LONDON : NEW YORK

Library of Congress
Catalog Card No. 74–80609

ISBN 0 7232 1539 1

Printed in Great Britain by
William Clowes & Sons, Limited
London, Beccles and Colchester
9.874

Contents

Preface   7

The Earliest Days   11

Steam Locomotives of the British Isles
  Arranged in Chronological Order from
  1837   17

Principal Museums with Static Locomotives
  on Display   181

Privately Owned Steam Engines   181

Fully Operational Lines   182

Index   185

Acknowledgements

Thanks are given to the following copyright owners and photographers for their kind permission to reproduce photographs in this book:

The Royal Scottish Museum, Edinburgh for page 10 (centre); British Rail for pages 10 (below), 15 (above), 17, 23, 33, 44 (centre), 54 (above), 66 (below), 71, 75 (below), 76, 123 (above), 140 (centre), 152, 158, 165 and 180; the Science Museum for pages 13 (above) and 44 (above); York Museum for pages 13 (centre) and 14; J. P. Mullett for page 30; W. A. Camwell for page 47; R. J. Buckley for pages 54 (centre), 101 and 123 (below); J. C. Haydon for page 78; R. A. Bowen for page 82; F. Moore for pages 92, 95, 96 and 103; D. A. Idle for page 98; R. C. Riley for pages 104 and 117; M. Mensing for page 110; P. B. Whitehouse for page 148 (above).

The majority of other photographs were taken by the author. In a few cases it has been impossible to trace the owners and we apologise for the infringement of any copyright.

Preface

The main purpose of this book is to present a brief outline of the history of the British steam locomotive from its earliest beginnings at the commencement of the 19th century. Its progressive development in the British Isles is followed until its official abandonment by the nationalized British Railways in 1968.

Within the confines of a small volume it is not possible to cover more than the barest essentials of such a wide subject. It has, however, been possible to include the principal landmarks and most important designs of locomotive which have developed over the period of a century and a half. Particular reference is made to types of which specimens have survived. These can still be seen at various museums and in the hands of the numerous preservation organizations which have grown up all over the country during the last few years. While many of these locomotives are static exhibits, there are quite a number of instances where locomotives can from time to time actually be found in steam, working over lengths of line varying from a few hundred yards to several miles of track. These occasions normally occur only during the summer months, and usually at weekends or during public holidays. Particulars of the more important of these are given on pages 181 to 183. On the whole, quite a large number of representative specimens of all ages have survived for posterity, and they provide a fairly complete general comprehensive picture. Inevitably there are some regrettable gaps of noted designs of the past which are missing. Some of these are of sufficient importance to be mentioned in this book to maintain the essential continuity, even though they are no longer in existence and consequently cannot be 'observed'. In one or two cases however there are excellent models which can be seen, especially at the Science Museum, South Kensington; British Railways also have some, until recently on view at Clapham and due to be transferred to York.

There are in all several hundred steam locomotives in existence in these islands. A few even still perform normal work at collieries and other industrial works, but their numbers are steadily diminishing owing to replacement by diesels or in some cases abandonment of rail traction altogether. Additionally there are several hundred shunting locomotives now in the hands of preservation societies and other organizations, or even owned by individuals. These are usually kept on private premises and are not available for inspection. It is quite impracticable to make more than a very brief reference to a few of these, or even to include every one of the main classes which have survived and are on exhibit.

It is an extraordinary fact that although it is now six years since BR dispensed entirely with steam operation (except for one small narrow gauge line in Wales) there are at the time of writing still some 200 engines to be found in the scrapyard of Messrs Woodhams at Barry. These have lain derelict for several years, gradually deteriorating owing to their exposure, but the owners have not yet decided to submit them to the blowtorch. Many of these locomotives have been eagerly sought after by the various preservation organizations with a view to restoration. Quite a number have been successfully acquired and delivered to various sites, at very great expense to the promoters, not only on account of the actual scrap value, but because of the heavy cost of transportation. Others may yet be saved, which explains the frequent reference to 'possibilities of others from Barry scrapyard' which will be found in the text.

The location of various preserved locomotives is not infrequently changed, and it may be that in a few instances such information has unavoidably become out of date by the time this book is published.

Some of the main line railways in the past have themselves on occasion set aside a notable locomotive for preservation, although this practice was not very widespread before nationalization in 1948. Many important locomotives which should have been retained were consigned ruthlessly to the scrap heap. Fortunately BR itself set up a committee during the 1950s to select typical designs, so far as they were still in existence, to form a national collection. Some of those thus set aside have never yet been on public view, although quite a number were to be seen at the former museum at Clapham, which has now closed. The exhibits, or most of them, will probably reappear at new premises at York that are now being adapted from the old steam shed there, and due to open in 1975. This building will provide much more accommodation, and will also absorb the exhibits from the earlier and smaller museum at York set up by the LNER in the 1930s, and not at present open to the public.

H. C. CASSERLEY *February 1974*

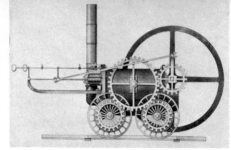

Model of
Trevithick's
engine of 1804,
the first steam
locomotive in
the world to
run on rails

Wylam Dilly,
the oldest
engine still in
existence

Puffing Billy, sister engine to *Wylam Dilly*. An old
picture taken while the engine was still at work, before
1862

The Earliest Days

To the average 'man in the street' who has no specialized knowledge of railway history, George Stephenson is often vaguely thought of as the inventor of the steam locomotive, but this is by no means the case. Nor was the famous *Rocket*, sometimes almost referred to as a sort of household name, the first engine to be built, or even *Locomotion No. 1*, four years older than the *Rocket*, but less well known.

Credit for building the first ever steam locomotive to run on rails must go to Richard Trevithick, who constructed an engine at Merthyr Tydfil in South Wales in 1804. After him came William Hedley, Timothy Hackworth, John Blenkinsop, and Matthew Murray, before George Stephenson got around to building his first engine for the Killingworth Colliery in 1814. The oldest steam locomotive still in existence, *Wylam Dilly*, was built in 1812 by William Hedley and Timothy Hackworth, at Wylam Colliery, Northumberland, for use on that colliery's lines. It ran until 1862, when it was presented to the Royal Scottish Museum, Edinburgh, where it can still be seen. A very similar engine, *Puffing Billy*, followed shortly afterwards, and this also has survived, and is now to be seen in the Science Museum, London.

Both of these had 3' 3" driving wheels, 9" × 36" cylinders, working pressure 50 lb and weighed about 8 tons, exclusive of the tender.

Next in order of longevity is an engine built by George Stephenson in 1822 for the Hetton Colliery,

Durham, for working the 8-mile 'main line' down to the coal staithes on the river Wear. After two rebuildings, in 1857 and 1882, it ran until 1912, when it was retained for preservation and eventually found a place in York Museum (temporarily closed at the time of writing but due to reopen in 1975). It led the procession of engines at the Darlington Centenary in 1925.

Driving wheels 3′ 0″ cylinders $10\frac{1}{4}″ \times 24″$ pressure 80 lb weight (including tender) $9\frac{3}{4}$ tons.

George Stephenson's famous *Locomotion No. 1*, which now stands on a pedestal at Bank Top station, Darlington, was built in 1825 for the Stockton & Darlington Railway, the first public passenger carrying line in the country to use steam traction. (The Oystermouth Tramway in South Wales, which later became the Swansea & Mumbles Railway, had opened in 1807, but for very many years only used horse traction.)

Locomotion No. 1 had 4′ 0″ driving wheels $9\frac{1}{2}″ \times 24″$ cylinders 50 lb pressure, and a weight of $6\frac{1}{2}$ tons. This engine also took part in the 1925 Centenary procession.

The famous Rainhill Trials on the Liverpool & Manchester Railway produced several contestants, among which was an engine built by Timothy Hackworth, *Sanspareil*, but it was excluded from taking part in the contest as it was slightly over the permitted weight. The locomotive is now to be found in the Science Museum, Kensington. It has 4′ 6″ driving wheels and 7″ × 18″ cylinders.

The winner of the trials was of course George Stephenson's *Rocket*. This engine's principal claim to fame lies not in the erroneous impression already mentioned that it was the first steam locomotive, but that it was the first to employ a tubular boiler, direct drive between the cylinder pistons and the crank pins on the driving wheels, and the use of a

(*left*) Hetton Colliery locomotive

(*centre*) Stockton & Darlington *Locomotion No. 1*

(*below*) Hackworth's *Sanspareil*

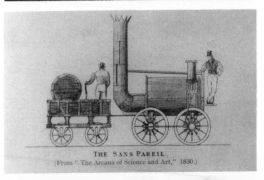

THE SANS PAREIL.
(From " The Arcana of Science and Art," 1830.)

George Stephenson's *Rocket*

blast pipe in the chimney—all essential basic features of the steam locomotive which was to last throughout much of its history. Apart from natural improvements, ·progressive enlargements over the years, and the introduction of such refinements as modern designs of valve gear, superheating, and the like, the ultimate steam locomotive as we know it was the direct development of its far-off ancestor, the *Rocket*. This engine had an interesting subsequent history. It last worked on the Brampton Railway in Cumberland before its retirement into the Science Museum, Kensington, and it was partially rebuilt with almost horizontal cylinders in place of the original ones inclined at about 45 degrees. There is a full-sized replica of it in its original condition which has been periodically on exhibition, and illustrations usually show the engine in this form. It has 4′ 8½″ driving wheels, 16½″ × 17″ cylinders, 50 lb pressure and weighs 4½ tons.

Shutt End Colliery *Agenoria*

Killingworth Colliery *Billy*

Canterbury & Whitstable Railway *Invicta*

Another survival of 1829 is an engine, *Agenoria*, built by Foster Rastrick & Co. of Stourbridge for the Earl of Dudley's Shutt End Colliery Railway, Kingswinford, Staffs. It worked until 1864, after which it appeared at the Science Museum, Kensington, but later became part of the collection housed at York. It has 4′ 0¾″ driving wheels, 8½″ × 36″ cylinders, and weighs 11 tons with tender.

This short review of very early existing specimens includes another Stephenson engine built about 1830 for the Killingworth Wagonway, believed to have at one time carried the name *Billy*, and now to be seen in Newcastle Municipal Museum.

Finally, in 1830, also appeared an engine built for the Canterbury & Whitstable Railway, *Invicta*. After about only ten years in service it was laid aside, but fortunately not broken up, and is now preserved in Canterbury Gardens. Like nearly all the other engines so far mentioned it was a 0–4–0 (except the *Rocket*, which is a 0–2–2) with 4′ 0″ driving wheels, 10″ × 18″ cylinders, 40 lb pressure and a weight of 6¼ tons.

1837 'North Star' Great Western Railway

One of the earliest and best known GWR broad gauge engines. It was one of two built in 1837 by R. Stephenson & Co. for the New Orleans Railway of the USA to the 5′ 6″ gauge, but never delivered. These engines were altered to 7′ 0″ gauge and purchased by the GWR, the first as *North Star* in 1837, and the second one, *Morning Star*, in 1839. Ten others of the same gauge, but differing in detail, appeared between 1839 and 1841. *Morning Star* was non-standard from the others in having 6′ 6″ driving wheels. The others were also named after stars, and most of these names reappeared many years later on Churchward 4-cylinder 4–6–0s.

North Star was reboiled in 1854 and worked

Replica of GWR broad gauge *North Star*

until 1871. On withdrawal it was preserved at Swindon, and it was joined in 1884 by one of the larger 4–2–2s, *Lord of the Isles*. Unfortunately, in 1906, an unforgivable act of ruthlessness caused these fine historic relics to be broken up. Some measure of atonement was made in 1925 by constructing a full-sized replica of the *North Star* as it was first built, although this could never be quite the same as the original machine.

Dimensions:
Driving wheels 7′ 0″   Leading and trailing wheels 4′ 0″   Cylinders 16″ × 16″   Weight 23 tons 7 cwt

Liverpool & Manchester Railway *Lion*

1838 'Lion' Liverpool and Manchester Railway

An early engine of the Liverpool and Manchester Railway built by Todd, Kitson & Laird in 1838. On withdrawal from active service in 1859 it was purchased by the Mersey Docks and Harbour Board for use as a stationary boiler. In this humble capacity it worked for many years, unknown to the railway world at large. Fortunately when the question of its replacement eventually came along in the 1920s it was 'discovered' and brought to the notice of the LMS authorities, who purchased it and restored it to its original condition in working order. Since then it has periodically been in steam on various occasions, and has been requisitioned more than once by a film company for appearance in an old-time railway scene. Of all the early engines, pre-1845, which have survived, this is almost the only one which has been seen by anyone within living memory working under its own steam. (*Derwent*—page 22—was steamed at the Darlington Centenary in 1925.)

Dimensions:
Driving wheels 5′ 0″   Cylinders 12″ × 18″   Pressure 50 lb

1840   Norris 4–2–0s

The earliest instance of engines being imported from abroad, which was a very rare occurrence in this country throughout the history of the steam locomotive. This usually happened only in time of urgent demand for more engine power which the home makers could not supply. An example is about 1899 when the Midland, Great Central and Great Northern all had to obtain some 2–6–0s from the USA. On the other hand, Great Britain, the country of origin of the steam locomotive, has exported many thousands of engines all over the world until quite recent times.

The little machines of 1840/1, 15 of which came from the firm of Norris in Philadelphia worked on the newly constructed Birmingham & Gloucester (later absorbed by the Midland) which line included the famous two-mile Lickey Incline with a gradient of 1 in 37. In spite of their small size they acquitted themselves very well; in fact, nine more of a slightly larger design were built in this country. All but the lightest trains very naturally had to be banked up the incline, a condition which persisted throughout the steam age. Incidentally, it was not one of these engines whose boiler exploded at Lickey on 11 November 1840, killing both driver and fireman. This is inferred from their tombstones still to be seen in Bromsgrove churchyard, and which embody very fine engraved replicas of the Norris 4–2–0s.

Dimensions:
Driving wheel 4′ 0″   Cylinders 10½″ × 18″

1845   LNWR 'Columbine'

The first engine to be built at Crewe works in 1845. Designed by Alexander Allan, a particular feature was the combination by graceful curves of outside cylinders and smokebox, and distinctive framing supporting the slide bars of the cylinders. These features were to be found on many subsequent designs, not only on the LNWR itself, but also on such diverse railways as the North London and the Highland, as late as the 1890s. *Columbine* finished up hauling the Engineering Department inspection saloon in 1902, and is now part of the collection at York Museum, at present temporarily closed, but due to reopen in 1975.

Dimensions:
Driving wheels 6′ 0″   Cylinders 15″ × 20″   Pressure 120 lb

Norris 4–2–0 for the Birmingham & Gloucester
Railway

LNWR *Columbine* at Wembley Exhibition in 1925

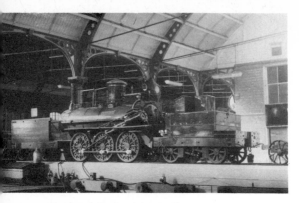

Stockton & Darlington No. 25 *Derwent*

1845 Stockton & Darlington 0–6–0

No. 25 *Derwent* was built by W. & A. Kitching in 1845 for the S&DR, and after a varied career came into the hands of the North Eastern in 1898, who retained it for preservation. An interesting and typical relic of the earliest age, it now stands on a plinth at Darlington station. It was steamed on the occasion of the 1925 Centenary.

Dimensions:
Driving wheels 4′ 0″ Cylinders 14½″ × 24″
Pressure 75 lb Weight 22 tons

1846 Bury Engines

The firm of Bury, Curtis & Kennedy, of which the founder was Mr Edward Bury, was responsible for the construction of a large number of engines during the 1830s and 1840s, the principal features being the use of inside cylinders, unusual for that period, and bar frames. The latter never caught on in this country, where plate frames became almost universal, although they became common practice abroad, particularly in the USA. The best known of Bury's engines were those he built for the London & Birmingham Railway. Fortunately two examples of his somewhat unique designs have survived, a 0–4–0 *Coppernob* for the Furness Railway, built in 1846, which worked until 1900, by which time it was the oldest engine still at work in the country. Latterly in Clapham Museum, it is not for the time being on public view.

Dimensions:
Driving wheels 4′ 9″ Cylinders 14″ × 24″ Pressure 100 lb

Furness Railway Bury engine No. 3 *Coppernob*

Another valuable survival is to be found in Ireland, a 2–2–2 built in 1848. After withdrawal in 1874 and after a long, precarious existence at Inchicore works of the Great Southern & Western Railway, its fate was more than once in doubt. However, it was rescued in a somewhat decrepit condition in the nick of time by Mr Bulleid, who went over to CIE in 1950 from British Railways, and it is now on permanent view at Cork station.

Dimensions:
Driving wheels 6' 0"   Cylinders 15" × 20"   Pressure 80 lb

1847   LNWR 'Cornwall'

Built by Francis Trevithick at Crewe in 1847, this engine underwent several transformations. At one time it was a 4–2–2, but it finally assumed its present form after a rebuild by Ramsbottom in 1858. In its last working days it was attached to a special saloon for use by the company's directors, on which duties it lasted until 1927.

Latterly housed in Clapham Museum until closure in 1973, it is not for the moment on public view.

It was rather unique in having driving wheels as large as 8' 6" diameter, not quite the largest ever used in this country (the old Bristol & Exeter had some 9' 0" engines), with 17½" cylinders and 140 lb pressure.

LNWR *Cornwall*

Padarn Railway *Fire Queen*

1848 Padarn Railway

Fire Queen is a somewhat extraordinary and very fortunate preservation of an early period. It is one of two engines built in 1848 by Horlock of Northfleet, Kent, for the 4′ 0″ gauge Padarn Railway, which was the main line from the Dinorwic slate quarries at Llanberis, North Wales (see page 65) to the coast.

Jenny Lind and *Fire Queen* worked until 1886, when they were replaced by more modern locomotives. Unusually for that period, the second one was not broken up, but placed in a shed which was bricked up, so that the engine was immovable. Here it remained for a period of 86 years! In 1969 the shed· was partially dismantled and this priceless relic removed to further safe keeping at the Penrhyn Castle Museum, Bangor.

1856 Long Boiler 0–6–0s

William Bouch's 0–6–0s for the Stockton & Darlington Railway developed from Stephenson's original
'long boiler' design. Usually known as the
'1001' class, these engines continued to be built
after amalgamation with the North Eastern. One
of them, No. 1275, which dates from 1874, survived
to be taken over by the LNER at the 1923 grouping.
It took part in the Darlington Centenary procession
in 1925 and was afterwards placed in York Museum
for permanent preservation.

Dimensions:
Driving wheels 5′ 6″ Cylinders 17″ × 26″ Pressure
130 lb

North Eastern long boiler 0–6–0 in York Museum

1857 Wantage Tramway 'Shannon'

This little engine has an unusually interesting
history. It was built by George England & Co. in
1857 for the Sandy & Potton Railway, and after

Wantage Tramway *Shannon* undergoing restoration in Swindon works, 1947

various ownerships eventually came into the hands of the Wantage Tramway, a rural roadside system in Berkshire. Here it worked until that line's closure in 1945. The Great Western took charge of it and renovated it for exhibition for a time at Wantage Road Station. It was later removed to the GWR Preservation Society's premises at Didcot.

Dimensions:
Driving wheels 3′ 0″   Cylinders 9″ × 12″   Pressure 120 lb   Weight 15 tons

1858   DX Goods

Almost the earliest example of standardization and mass production of locomotives on a large scale. The first of these 0–6–0 freight engines was built by John Ramsbottom for the London & North Western Railway in 1858, and between that date and 1872 no fewer than 857 of them were built. In addition, another 86 were constructed at Crewe for the Lancashire & Yorkshire during 1871–4. This total of 943 absolutely identical engines of one type is a record which has never been exceeded in quite the

LNWR Webb DX goods, built 1858, scrapped 1928

same way. Very similar records were to be found later on the Midland, and also in more recent years, as will be recounted later.

Of simple and light construction, they put in many years of hard work, and no fewer than 88 of them were still in existence in 1923 at the grouping. These were allocated Nos. 8000–8087 in the LMS list, but not many of them survived to carry their new numbers. The last to run was No. 8084, which was withdrawn in 1930. They changed little during their long life. Webb had rebuilt them with slightly larger boilers and provided them with cabs, which they lacked when originally built. The first 54 engines had carried names, but these were all removed in 1864. Regrettably, none of them survived into the later preservation age.

Dimensions:
Driving wheels 5′ 2″   Cylinders 17″ × 24″   Pressure 120 lb

1863   Beattie 2–4–0Ts

An early type of engine for local passenger work on the London & South Western, of which 85 were

LSWR Beattie 2–4–0T

built between 1863 and 1875, by Joseph Beattie and by his son, W. G. Beattie, who followed him in 1871. Most of them spent about 20 years on the various suburban lines out of Waterloo, but a few were to be found in other areas such as the Exeter and Exmouth branch. The London ones also migrated to the country when displaced by Adams 4–4–2Ts in the 1880s (see page 62). From 1888 onwards they were gradually taken out of service, and all had gone by 1898, with three exceptions. These, remarkably, were destined to enjoy working lives some three times longer than any of their sisters. The reason for their retention lay in the fact that for very many years they were the only engines found to be suitable for the Wenford Bridge mineral line in Cornwall. Here they spent the rest of their existence until finally displaced at the end of 1962, for a short time by small GWR 0–6–0PTs and ultimately by diesels.

The three engines in question originally 298, 314 and 329, were reboilered and renewed several times, but without much change in appearance. They ultimately became BR 30587, 30585 and 30586 respectively. Fortunately two have survived, 30587, officially preserved, but not at present on public view, and 30585 in working order at Quainton Road.

Dimensions:
Driving wheels 5′ 7″   Cylinders 16½″ × 22″   Pressure 160 lb

1864   Beyer, Peacock 4–4–0Ts

A standard design of engine evolved by Beyer, Peacock for working the early underground railways in London. In all, 66 were built for the Metropolitan Railway and 54 for the District Railway down to the year 1886. Another 28 were acquired by the LNWR, Midland and LSWR.

When the underground lines were electrified in the early part of the century most of the engines were scrapped. However, the Metropolitan retained a few for various duties, and the District kept two for departmental use, one of which lasted until 1932. The country Brill branch of the Metropolitan was worked by two or three of the remaining ones until closure in 1935, and the few survivors were all scrapped in 1936, except No. 23 (latterly London Transport L45) which was retained for preservation. Fully restored to original condition,

Beyer, Peacock Metropolitan 4–4–0T as restored to original condition

it was in Clapham Museum for some years, but it is now with the London Transport collection at Syon Park, Isleworth.

Dimensions:
Driving wheels 5′ 9″   Cylinders 17″ × 24″   Pressure 160 lb

1865 'Dolgoch'—Talyllyn Railway

This 0–4–0 well tank engine was built by Fletcher Jennings & Co. in 1865, and together with a second locomotive, a 0–4–2ST, worked the whole of the traffic for a period of 87 years until 1951.   The railway, then threatened with extinction, was taken over by the Talyllyn Preservation Society, the first of its kind in the world, but whose example has been followed by numerous other organizations of a similar nature. *Dolgoch* attained its working centenary in 1965, and together with its sister *Tal-y-llyn* still takes an active part in the working of the railway, but these two veterans are now reinforced by other acquisitions to the locomotive stock.

Dimensions:
Gauge of railway 2′ 3″   Driving wheels 2′ 3″ Cylinders 8″ × 15″   Pressure 70 lb   Weight 8½ tons

Talyllyn Railway *Dolgoch*

1866 Midland Railway Kirtley Engines

Matthew Kirtley was the first locomotive engineer of the Midland Railway from its formation in 1844 until he was succeeded by Mr S. W. Johnson in 1873. He had previously served on the Stockton & Darlington Railway, Liverpool & Manchester, the London & Birmingham Railway, and the Birmingham & Derby Junction, one of the constituents of the Midland, and had in consequence been associated with early public railways right from the beginning. It is not always generally realized the considerable influence Mr Kirtley had on the development of the steam locomotive. He was for instance instrumental in designing a firebox in which ordinary coal could be burnt satisfactorily; up to that time, the early 1860s, coke had been the ordinary fuel. He was also the pioneer of standardization, even anticipating Mr Johnson, and F. W. Webb on the LNWR, as mentioned elsewhere, in this respect. All of Kirtley's engines had one common feature—the use of outside frames. His passenger engines were 2–2–2s, the last of which came out in 1866, and 2–4–0s, with several hundred 0–6–0s for freight duties. He also produced a smaller number of tank engines of 0–4–4T and 0–6–0T wheel arrangement; one of the latter built at Derby in 1855 lasted until 1920, and another from 1863 to as late as 1928. These extreme examples were somewhat unusual although not all that overlong by Kirtley and general Midland standards. Here the record was held by a 2–4–0 built at Derby in 1866, which achieved a working life of no fewer than 82 years, during which time she had been reboilered at least four times. Thanks to the efforts of the Stephenson Locomotive Society, through the medium of Mr D. S. Barrie, and in which the present author can modestly

Midland Railway Kirtley 2–4–0

claim his active part, she was saved from the breakers on withdrawal in 1947. She was restored to pre-1907 condition in MR colours with her old number 158A, which she had carried prior to that date. At the 1907 renumbering she had become No. 2, later to be 20002, which she carried in her last working days. She is a very fortunate survival of a period rather thinly represented in the preservation field. This locomotive is now housed temporarily in the old tram depot at Stoneygate, Leicester, along with Johnson single wheeler No. 118 (see page 70). The exhibition is open to visitors at certain restricted times, but the engine will eventually be on display at the main museum in Leicester itself which is now being reconstructed to accommodate several other engines.

Dimensions:
Driving wheels 6′ 3″   Cylinders 18″ × 24″   Pressure 140 lb

1866   Great Southern & Western 0–6–0s

Designed by Alexander MacDonnell, this was the only class of engine on any Irish railway which was built in sufficient numbers to be regarded as a standard type. Even then the total number built, 111 in all, was small by English standards; the class was perpetuated a few at a time over a long period by three of Mr MacDonnell's successors, the last not coming out until 1903.

They were true mixed traffic engines, 'maids of all work' in every sense, being seen all over the system and some lasting until the end of steam in the 1960s. In later years many were rebuilt with Belpaire fireboxes, superheaters, and extended smokeboxes, but otherwise they changed little during their long lives.

Two have survived, No. 184, unrebuilt, officially preserved by CIE, and No. 186 superheated, by the Irish Railway Preservation Society in Northern Ireland, whose headquarters are at Whitehead near Belfast. The engine is maintained in working order and is frequently used on enthusiasts' excursions. In fact, as recently as September 1973, this veteran of 1879, nearing its century, gallantly worked almost unaided a 400-mile all steam tour on a round trip from Dublin, with an overnight stay in Waterford.

Dimensions:
Driving wheels 5′ 2″   Cylinders 18″ × 24″   Pressure 160 lb

Great Southern & Western Railway. Restored 0–6–0 No. 186 of 1879 at Kilkenny in September 1973 whilst working a 400 mile two-day all-steam rail tour

North Eastern Railway *Aerolite*

1869 'Aerolite'   North Eastern Railway

Some authorities regard this interesting engine as dating back to the year 1851, but although there was an engine constructed in that year bearing the same name, it can really only be regarded as an ancestor of the 1869 machine, which was an entirely new locomotive. It was built by E. Fletcher as a 2–2–2 well tank with sandwich pattern outside frames. Its various features characteristic of Fletcher's practice were the plain stove-pipe chimney and large dome with Salter spring balance safety valves. In 1886 it was rebuilt by T. W. Worsdell as a side tank with new frames and was completely altered in appearance. At this period it was numbered 66 and lost its name. It ran in this form for only six years, and was rebuilt again by Wilson Worsdell in 1892, this time as a Worsdell-von-Borries 2 cylinder compound. At the same time a leading bogie was added, making it a 4–2–2T. As such it was a very handsome little engine. In 1902 it was once again rebuilt, this time the wheel arrangement being reversed, and in its final form it became a 2–2–4T. At the same time its name *Aerolite* was restored. It ran thus until 1933, usually being employed in hauling an officers' inspection saloon.   On withdrawal the LNER repainted it in North Eastern colours and placed it in York Museum.

	Original condition	First rebuild as 2-2-2T	As 4-2-2T	As 2-2-4T
Driving wheels	5′ 6″	5′ 7¾″	5′ 7¾″	5′ 7¾″
Cylinders	13″ × 20″	13″ × 20″	(1) 13″ × 20″ (1) 18½″ × 20″	(1) 13″ × 20″ (1) 18½″ × 20″
Pressure	—	140 lb	160 lb	175 lb

Festiniog Railway Fairlie double ended locomotive

1869   Fairlie Engines

The Festiniog Railway with an ancient history dating back to 1836 was the first in the field of the narrow gauge, the dimension which it adopted being the narrow measurement of 1′ 11½″.   Steam traction was introduced in 1863, with some 4-coupled saddle tank engines.   The main purpose of this railway had been to carry slate from the large deposits in the area around Blaenau Ffestiniog down to the small seaport of Portmadoc for shipment.   By 1869 more powerful engines had become necessary, and the first of a type of double engine with two boilers and sets of driving wheels appeared.   This had a central cab, and a single firebox common to both boilers.   The design was known as Fairlie's patent, the origins of which went back to 1852 when such a locomotive had appeared in Austria. It was later to be used in many parts of the world on both broad and narrow gauge. Four such engines duly appeared on the Festiniog Railway, and two of them are still in working order on this busy pleasure railway which operates throughout the summer season. This railway was closed in 1946 and partly reopened in the 1950s. It is now actively engaged in the restoration of the whole 13-mile route up to Blaenau Ffestiniog. The two surviving Fairlies are No. 10 *Merddin Emrys* built in 1879 and 3 *Earl of Merioneth* of 1885.

Dimensions:
Driving wheels 2′ 9¼″   Cylinders (2 pairs) 9″ × 14″
Pressure 160 lb

1870   Great Northern Stirling 8 Footers

Patrick Stirling's famous 4–2–2s were introduced in 1870 and for nearly 30 years worked alongside his 2–2–2s. These were on the main line expresses between London and York.

They were the only engines that Stirling built either with a leading bogie or with outside cylinders. Fifty-three of them appeared up to 1894, with some increase in dimensions and weight in the later series.

GNR No. 1 brought out from York Museum working an early enthusiasts' special train through Finsbury Park in 1938

Two of them No. 668 and 775, distinguished themselves in the Races to the North in 1888 and 1895. The last in regular traffic was taken out of service in 1916, but the original engine, the well-known No. 1 of 1870, worked until 1907 and had been preserved for many years in Kings Cross shed.

In 1938 it was put into steam and worked on special trains between Kings Cross and Grantham or Cambridge. It was eventually placed in York Museum, where it still is, but not at present on public view until the new premises open in 1975.

Dimensions:
Driving wheels 8′ 1″ Cylinders 18″ × 28″ Pressure 140 lb Weight 38½ tons, of which 15 tons is on the driving wheels.

1872 Stroudley 0-6-0T 'Terriers'

The origin of these well-known engines lay, not in the London Brighton & South Coast, on which line they attained their fame, but in the far north of Scotland on the Highland Railway. Here Mr William Stroudley was Locomotive Superintendent for about three years, between 1866 and 1869, before taking up his appointment with the LB&SCR on which he was to become so well known.

While on the HR he built three small 0-6-0Ts which were the direct antecedents of his famous class on the Brighton, and bore several distinctive features, such as the design of the cab, which were to be repeated in the later engines. Like their successors, they were extremely long lived and lasted well into LMS days, the last of them surviving until 1932.

In all, 50 engines were turned out from Brighton works between 1872 and 1880. They had an interesting and varied history, much too involved to

Stroudley Terrier No. 32636, one of the last in regular service in 1962, now on the Bluebell Railway restored as LB&SCR *Fenchurch*

be repeated here, but this has already been amply recorded elsewhere in detail. It is enough to say that although some of them were taken out of service as early as 1900, a few were scrapped and others sold out of service to other railways. This practice continued over many years and many engines enjoyed long lives indeed. More than 20 were absorbed into the Southern Railway at the grouping in 1923, and nearly all of them were destined to become part of British Railway's stock at nationalization in 1948; of these several remained in service until 1963. By this time the preservation movement was well under way, and these hardy little lightweight engines were much sought after by various bodies.

The net result is that no fewer than ten out of the original 50 are still in existence, some as static exhibits and others in working order. They underwent little change over the years, the most important being the provision of new boilers, embodying extended smokeboxes which upgraded them from their original classification of A1 to A1x. Practically all of the late survivors were so treated.

They were originally painted in the well-known yellow livery of the old LB&SCR (known as

'Stroudley's improved engine green) and all bore names of localities on the Brighton system. These were removed by D. Earle Marsh from 1905 onwards, and they assumed the dark brown hue introduced by that gentleman, to be in turn eventually replaced by Southern green and BR lined out black. Many of the survivors have been restored to the original yellow livery, and have had their names reinstated.

The survivors may be summarized as follows:

82 *Boxhill* Officially preserved by SR. Was in Clapham Museum, but not at present on public view.

55 *Stepney* In working order on the Bluebell Railway.

72 *Fenchurch* In working order on the Bluebell Railway.

54 *Waddon* Canadian Railroad Museum, Montreal.

40 formerly *Brighton* Now preserved in the Isle of Wight (it had been sold to the Isle of Wight Central Railway in 1902). It was exhibited at the Paris Exhibition in 1878 and obtained a gold medal.

78 Formerly *Knowle* Now exhibited at Butlin's Holiday Camp, Minehead as BR 32678.

62 Formerly *Martello* At Bressingham Hall, Diss as BR32662.

46 *Newington* Static exhibit outside the Hayling Billy public house, Hayling Island.

70 formerly *Poplar* Now restored as Kent & East Sussex No. 3 *Bodiam* (to which railway it had been sold in 1901) at Tenterden.

50 originally *Whitechapel* Now Kent & East Sussex No. 10 *Sutton* at Tenterden.

Dimensions:

Driving wheels 4' 0" Cylinders 12" × 20" Pressure 150 lb Weight 28¼ tons

1872 Fletcher 2–4–0s

Mr E. Fletcher was locomotive superintendent of the North Eastern Railway from 1854 until 1883, during which time he built a number of 2–4–0s for passenger work. There were 54 of a large main line type for express duties, the '901' class, of which No. 910, which ran until 1925, is preserved in York Museum (not due to reopen to the public until 1975).

Dimensions:
Driving wheels 7′ 1¼″ Cylinders 17″ × 24″ Pressure 140 lb

1873 Beyer, Peacock 2–4–0Ts

In 1873 this firm built the first of a series of engines for the 3′ 0″ gauge Isle of Man Railway, eventually to total 15 examples, the last of them coming out in 1926, by which time the dimensions had slightly increased. At the time of writing a portion of this railway is still in operation. It was reopened in 1967 after temporary closure, and is supported privately, with help from the Manx Government, but its future is precarious.

NER Fletcher 2–4–0 in York Museum

Beyer, Peacock design of 2–4–0T for the Isle of Man Railway

All of the engines, Nos. 1–14 and 16, are still in existence, although only about four are actually in use; others have not worked for several years, and some are in a more or less derelict condition although safely housed in a shed.

Dimensions
Driving wheels 3′ 9″   Cylinders 11″ × 18″   Pressure 160 lb   Weight 18¼ tons

A similar engine was supplied in 1878 to the Ballymena and Larne Railway, in Ireland. It was sold in 1928 by the LMS, its later owner, to the Castlederg & Victoria Bridge Railway, and scrapped on the closure of that line in 1934.

1874   Industrial Locomotives

It is not possible to mention more than very briefly the countless number of engines built for industrial use at collieries, steelworks, and all manner of other works to be found all over the country. Some of these are still found using steam locomotives, although in ever decreasing numbers, either because they are being displaced by diesel or, regrettably, on account of the closing down of the works or abandonment of rail traction.

Generally representative of these engines is *Bauxite*, to be seen in the Science Museum, Kensington. It was built by the old firm of Black Hawthorn in 1874 and latterly owned by the Industrial Aluminium Company Limited at Hebburn Chemical works.

Among the many builders of locomotives for this type of work should be mentioned the Avonside Engine Co., Bristol; W. G. Bagnall Ltd., Stafford: Andrew Barclay & Son, Kilmarnock; Beyer, Peacock of Manchester; Dübs & Co., Glasgow; Hawthorn Leslie & Co., Newcastle; Hudswell Clarke, of Leeds; Hunslet Engine Co., Leeds; Kerr Stuart & Co., Stoke on Trent; Kitson & Co., Leeds; Manning Wardle, of Leeds; Neilson & Co., Glasgow; Peckett & Sons, Bristol; Stephenson & Hawthorns, Newcastle; Yorkshire Engine Co., Sheffield. Other firms are either no longer in existence or have abandoned the almost extinct craft of steam locomotive building. However, numerous examples of engines which came from the works of these companies are to be found up and down the country in the hands of various preservation societies and individuals.

1874   Webb's LNWR Passenger Engines

The 2–4–0 'Precedent' design of F. W. Webb was his most successful passenger class. Although he seems to have been far more interested in his subsequent experiments in compounding, the 'Precedents' were the only really reliable express engines that the North Western possessed until Whale's *Precursor* appeared in 1904. The latter may be regarded as a very much enlarged version of the 'Precedents'.

The class consisted in the first place of 90 engines built between 1874 and 1882. Subsequently,

Bauxite, a typical industrial locomotive, now in the Science Museum

LNWR Webb 2–4–0 *Hardwicke*

LNWR Webb compound No. 509 *Ajax*

between 1887 and 1894, 96 engines of an older class of 2-4-0, built by John Ramsbottom from 1866 onwards, the 'Newtons', were entirely renewed in conformity with the Webb engines. It was not until later years that the sterling worth of these remarkable locomotives came to be realized; some of their prodigious feats of haulage, considering their small size, have probably seldom been equalled elsewhere. As was to be expected, their coal consumption was high when greatly overloaded but nevertheless they were capable of 'doing the job' when called upon, as they frequently were.

Two of the best known were No. 955 *Charles Dickens*, which put in a total mileage of over 2,300,000 between its construction in 1882 and withdrawal in 1912, and No. 790 *Hardwicke*, which distinguished itself in the 1895 race to Scotland. This engine was preserved by the LMS Railway and was more recently in Clapham Museum, but for the time being it is not on public view.

Eighty of the class survived to be absorbed into the LMS at the grouping, and were allocated Nos. 5000–5079 in the LMS list, although about half of them did not last long enough to carry these numbers. The last in service was No. 5001 *Snowdon*, which ran for its last few months in 1934 as No. 25001, as the new class 5 4–6–0s were then beginning to appear, and were taking the numbers 5000 upwards.

Dimensions:
Driving wheels 6' 9"   Cylinders 17" × 24"   Pressure 140 lb (later 150 lb)

Concurrently with the building of his much more successful simple engines, Webb embarked on a full-scale production of 3 cylinder compounds with uncoupled wheels. These were in effect double single wheelers, in which two high pressure cylinders drove the rear driving wheels, and one large low pressure cylinder, into which the steam was exhausted through an intermediate chamber, activated the front pair.   The absence of coupling rods meant that one pair of wheels could slip without the other, resulting in the receiver becoming choked if the rear wheels were slipping, or denuded of steam when the front pair ran away with themselves.   It was not unknown even for the respective driving wheels to be revolving in opposite directions when the engine was attempting to start.   In spite of these handicaps the later engines were capable of quite good work when they really got going, and undoubtedly the best of them all was a class of ten, built in 1889 and 1890, known as the 'Teutonics'. These also were 2–2–2–0s, but larger than their predecessors, with 7′ 0″ driving wheels.   No. 1301 *Teutonic* was the first engine, and was followed by nine others, bearing the numbers 1302–1307, 1309 and 1311–1312.   The most famous of these was No. 1304 *Jeanie Deans*, which worked the 2.0 pm 'Corridor' from Euston to Crewe, returning with the up 7.32 express, almost continuously from 1891 to 1899.   No. 1309 *Adriatic* took part in the 1895 race to Scotland, its finest effort being to cover the $133\frac{1}{2}$ miles to Stafford in 127 minutes.   Here a stop had to be made for water, and despite a delay there of $3\frac{1}{2}$ minutes, it reached Crewe (158 miles) in $156\frac{1}{2}$ minutes, and this with a load of four bogie coaches, about 95 tons.   Despite the comparative success of the 'Teutonics', they were all swept away along with their brethren when Webb retired in 1903, and his place was taken by George Whale. The 2–2–2–0 engines, which were in effect an uncoupled version of the 2–4–0 type, were supplemented by some larger 2–2–2–2s, here the equivalent of a more conventional 2–4–2.   This wheel arrangement has never been used by a standard gauge line railway in this country, although it was to be found at one time on the Continent, notably in Belgium and France. Some of these later 2–2–2–2s lingered after the rapid demise of the 2–2–2–0s, and operated until 1912, but it need hardly be said that none of these classes survived for preservation, although there is a fine model to be found in the Science Museum, Kensington.

The story of Webb's ill-fated LNWR compounds has been told many times and it is too lengthy to go into in more detail here. It may be mentioned that apart from a few miscellaneous tank engines and a considerable number of 0–8–0 engines for freight duties, with both 3 and 4 cylinders, he continued his experiments in 1897 by turning out two 4-cylinder 4–4–0s (see page 86) one a simple and the other a compound, to be tested one against the other. Not surprisingly, Mr Webb came down in favour of the compound version, and 38 more were built in 1899 and 1900, followed by another 40 of slightly enlarged dimensions between 1901 and 1903. Of this total of 80, all but three came into the hands of the LMS in 1923, and nearly all by that time had been converted to simple versions with two inside cylinders only, although one remained as a compound until it was scrapped in 1928. The whole class had disappeared by the end of 1931.

The last Whale 'Precursor' No. 25297 *Sirocco*

The most efficient passenger engines the LNWR ever had were undoubtedly Mr Whale's 'Precursors', 4-4-0s, of 1904, of which 130 were built, and the superheated version, the 'George the Fifths', introduced by his successor, Mr C. J. Bowen-Cooke in 1910—another 90 engines. Numerous 4-6-0s built concurrently with 4-4-0s and in later years culminating in the 4 cylinder 'Claughtons', although adequate, never quite attained the same brilliance, at any rate comparing size for size.

It was unfortunate that although one Precursor just lasted into BR days, and it was hoped that it might have been preserved, this did not come about. In fact the only LNWR engine of this century to survive is the 0-8-0 mentioned on page 77.

1874 Johnson and Fowler 0–6–0Ts

The history of this class and its subsequent developments is a long one extending over a period of some 58 years. This was S. W. Johnson's first design after coming to the Midland Railway in 1873. 25 of these engines were built initially by Neilson & Co in 1874-5, and another 15 by the Vulcan Foundry in 1875-6. Many more followed from Derby between 1878 and 1893, and still further batches from outside builders until 1899, by which

Midland Railway Johnson 0–6–0T

The final LMS development of the original Johnson design of 1874

time the class totalled 280 engines. Prior to 1907 their numbers were somewhat scattered, but in that year they became Nos. 1620–1899. A further 60 engines of a slightly enlarged version came from the Vulcan Foundry from 1899–1902, later Nos. 1900–1959. Many of these were fitted with condensing apparatus for working over the 'widened' lines of the Metropolitan Railway, and these subsequently spent a lot of their working lives in the London area. The MR had evidently by 1902 a sufficient stock of shunting tank engines, and no more were built by that company, but the design in a slightly improved form reappeared again under LMS auspices as one of their standard types. No fewer than 415 were built between 1924 and 1931, as well as a further seven for the Somerset & Dorset Railway; these engines later became merged into LMS stock.

During the 1930s Nos. 1900–59 were renumbered 7200–7259. All of the Midland engines at first carried Johnson's distinctive boiler and the Salter safety valve in the dome, but most of the later ones to survive, and all of the 1900–1959 batch, gradually acquired Belpaire type boilers. The earlier engines had only half section cabs, which some retained even after rebuilding with Belpaire boilers. All lasted

49

until the early 1920s, when some were taken out of service, but 95 of the original series, and all of the '1900' class, survived to be taken into BR stock, and to have their numbers increased by 40000.

The LMS-built engines were eventually re-numbered into one series as 7260–7681; this included the seven engines from the Somerset & Dorset Railway. All survived to become BR 47260–47681, and some of them were still at work during the last years of steam. Several have survived for preservation, including four, Nos. 47327, 47357, 47445 and 47564 acquired by the preservation society now known as the Midland Railway. Co. Ltd., which intends to operate a length of track at Swanwick, near Derby. No. 47357 has already been restored in working order with its original LMS number 16440. No. 47383 is to be found on the Severn Valley Railway, and others are in prospect from Barry scrapyard.

On a still happier note, one of the original Johnsons has survived, No. 1708, which has been secured by the Keighley & Worth Valley Railway, a very suitable venue, as this type of engine was once in regular service on the Oxenhope branch. It is one of the earliest engines, originally built in 1880 as No. 1418, renumbered 1708 in 1907, and even-

The original Johnson type of goods engine introduced to the Midland Railway in 1875

tually BR 41708.   It was one of half a dozen which
outlasted their sisters in being specially retained for
shunting at Staveley Ironworks until these were
turned over to diesels in 1965.   On withdrawal
these were among the oldest engines still running on
British Railways, and efforts to secure preservation
of one of them were fortunately successful.

Dimensions of original engines:
Driving wheels 4′ 7″   Cylinders 17″ × 24″   Pressure
140 lb

Dimensions of ultimate Fowler LMS engines:
Driving wheels 4′ 7″   Cylinders 18″ × 26″   Pressure
160 lb

1875   Johnson, Deeley and Fowler o–6–os

The history of these classes follows somewhat
parallel lines to that of the tank engines just described, except that it covers an even longer period
and the gradual development was more marked.
Broadly speaking, there were three main varieties,
the two later ones being nothing more than larger
versions of the original basic design, of which the
first 140 were turned out in the space of three years,
from 1875–7.   The class was multiplied at intervals
until 1902, by which time a total of no fewer than
865 had appeared, plus another 40 built for the
Somerset & Dorset Joint Railway, and 16 more for
the Midland & Great Northern Joint.   Some had
4′ 11″ driving wheels instead of the normal 5′ 3″,
but this was the only marked deviation.   Apart from
the Webb DX o–6–os on the LNWR mentioned on
page 27, it was the first instance of standardization
on a large scale.   The designer, Mr S. W. Johnson,
who took over the post of Chief Mechanical Engineer for the Midland Railway in 1873, can rightly
be regarded, along with Mr F. W. Webb of the

North Western, as being the chief innovator. It was not until well into this century that the construction of such large numbers of locomotives of one design became common practice.

The main pattern of development divides itself into three distinct categories. The original 1875 design, which eventually became class 2 in the MR power classification introduced in later years, remained standard right up to 1902, and was modified by Mr R. M. Deeley in 1903 with the provision of a much larger boiler, which brought the new engine into the class 3 category. Many of the earlier engines were rebuilt to conform, although some remained as class 2 throughout their existence. They were usually modified with the provision of a Belpaire firebox and Ross pop safety valves in place of the old Johnson Salter spring balance mounted on the dome. The class 3s also eventually received Belpaire fireboxes.

Finally, Sir Henry Fowler brought out the considerably enlarged class 4 in 1911, with a further increase in boiler dimensions. These were also superheated. For several years there were only two of these engines, but construction was resumed in 1917 and proceeded steadily not only through the rest of the Midland's existence to 1922, but was adopted as standard for the newly formed London Midland & Scottish. This railway continued to turn them out as late as 1940, by which time there were no fewer than 772 of them, numbered 3835 to 4606, including five that had been built for the Somerset & Dorset.

These engines were usually referred to in general terms as the class 4 goods, although in actual fact they did a lot of passenger work of a semi main line character, such as excursion and relief holiday trains, and were always an invaluable and useful standby in an emergency.

Of the Johnson and Deeley classes 2 and 3 there were ultimately 935 examples on the parent system, Nos. 2900–3834, plus another 56 on the S&DJR and M&GNJR; the grand total of 1763 for all these subdivisions of the class as a whole represents the greatest number of a single basic design which has ever occurred in this country. The only possible comparison would be the Great Western saddle and pannier tanks, but these were of too many diversified varieties to be considered as of one general class.

It is most unfortunate that none of the original Johnson and Deeley engines has survived, although a few ran as late as 1964, but two of the Fowlers have been preserved with the possibility of one or even two more from Barry scrapyard.

The two definitely preserved are No. 4027, the first to be built under the LMS régime in 1924, and one of the original Midland engines, No. 3924 of 1920, now to be found on the Keighley & Worth Valley Railway.

Principal dimensions

Class 2
Driving wheels 5′ 3″* Cylinders 18″ × 26″ Pressure 160 lb

Class 3
Driving wheels 5′ 3″* Cylinders 18″ × 26″ Pressure 160 lb

Class 4
Driving wheels 5′ 3″ Cylinders 20″ × 26″ Pressure 175 lb

It may be mentioned that *class 1* comprised an earlier double framed 0-6-0 of Johnson's predecessor, William Kirtley, of which again several hundred were built between 1850 and 1874. Like nearly all Midland engines, they were exceptionally

* Some engines had 4′ 11″ driving wheels.

Final development of the MR standard freight engine, built in large numbers between 1911 and 1940

(*above*) Lancashire & Yorkshire Railway Barton Wright 0–6–0 tender engine
(*below*) The same design, rebuilt as saddle tank

long lived, and the last did not disappear until 1949.

The 0–6–0 tender engine was such a popular universal type that it was used with varying degrees, but generally in very considerable numbers by every company in the British Isles which employed tender engines, with one rather curious exception, the Great North of Scotland. If, however, it would be possible to name any particular railway as an out and out 0–6–0 line for freight and general duties, it would undoubtedly have to be the Midland.

1876 Lancashire & Yorkshire Rly, Barton Wright 0–6–0 & 0–6–0STs

Barton Wright's standard goods engine for the L&YR, of which 280 were built between 1876 and 1887.

When Aspinall became CME at Horwich he introduced his own design of 0–6–0, and these were constructed in considerable numbers. As there was an acute shortage of shunting engines, he proceeded to rebuild most of the earlier Barton Wright engines with saddle tanks. Between 1891 and 1900 the whole of the earlier members of the class had been thus dealt with, but the final 50 remained as tender engines. All of them, both rebuilt and unrebuilt, passed into LMS hands in 1923, the saddle tanks becoming Nos. 11303–11532, and the tender engines 12015–12064. 96 of the former and 25 of the latter were still in service at nationalization, many surviving to have 40000 added to their numbers. The last surviving 0–6–0, No. 52044, was not withdrawn until 1959; this engine and one of the saddle tanks have both been secured by the Keighley & Worth Valley Railway, and can be seen at Haworth or Oxenhope.

The 0–6–0 has been restored as L&YR 957 in its

old colours.   The saddle tank, which had become LMS 11456, had been sold out of service in 1937 to a colliery near Wigan, and on withdrawal in 1967 was rescued from the National Coal Board who were willing to make it available for preservation.   It has been restored to its old condition as L&YR 752.

Principal dimensions, applicable to both varieties: Driving wheels 4′ 6″ Cylinders 17$\frac{1}{2}$″ × 26″ Pressure 140 lb

1877   Vertical Boiler Locomotives

Usually nicknamed 'Coffee pots', this type of small engine with a vertical boiler was much used by some industrial concerns, particularly in quarries and the like, from the latter years of the 19th century onwards, and in a few cases until comparatively recent times.   Three firms which specialized in these locomotives were de Winton & Co. of Caernarvon, Alexander Chaplin & Co. of Glasgow, and Head, Wrightson & Company Limited of Thornaby-on-Tees.

Several specimens have survived for preservation, mostly as static exhibits in various industrial museums, one being at Towyn, North Wales, and others in the north east.   *Chaloner*, built by de Winton in 1877 for the Penrhyn Railway, was later transferred to the Pen-y-Orsedd Quarries, North Wales, where it worked until the 1950s.   It may now be seen occasionally in steam and working trains on the 2′ 0″ gauge Leighton Buzzard Railway, Beds.

A curious survival of the GWR 7′ 0″ gauge is *Tiny*, built in 1868 for the South Devon Railway. It is to be found on a plinth on one of the platforms at Newton Abbot station.   The vertical boiler is anything but typical of the broad gauge era of that railway.   (Brunel's 7′ 0″ gauge was abandoned in

Vertical boiler locomotive *Chaloner* on the Leighton Buzzard Light Railway

1892.) Unfortunately, it is the only genuine broad gauge engine still in existence, as *North Star* (detailed on page 17) is but a replica of the original.

Dimensions of 'Chaloner':
Driving wheels 1′ 8″   Cylinders 6″ × 12″   Pressure 80 lb

1878 0–4–4T Swindon Marlborough & Andover Railway

This engine is of historic importance as it was the first British locomotive to be fitted with Walschaert's valve gear. It was also unusual in that it was a single Fairlie engine, the coupled wheels and cylinders forming a separate forward bogie. It should have been a very flexible machine on curves, but in other respects it was far from successful. Its valve gear was not properly understood by the engineers into whose hands it came, and it was very heavy on coal, even on light trains. Walschaert's gear was not used again in Great Britain until the 1890s, when it was applied to some Worsdell-von-Borries compounds on the North Eastern and Belfast and Northern Counties Railways. In more recent years it was adopted extensively.

After a few years of comparative inactivity the engine quietly disappeared. Its owners, the Swindon, Marlborough & Andover Railway later became the Midland & South Western Junction, which was absorbed into the GWR at the grouping. The illustration is the only known one of the engine, from a photograph probably taken about 1880. The plate resting on the running plate bears the inscription 'Fairlie's Patent'.

Dimensions:
Driving wheels 5′ 6″   Trailing wheels 4′ 0″   Cylinders 16″ × 22″   Weight 44 tons

SM&AR Fairlie engine, with Walschaert's valve gear

1880   London Tilbury & Southend
Railway 4–4–2Ts

From 1880 onwards the outside cylindered 4–4–2T was the standard type for the heavy outer suburban traffic of the LTSR, successive designs being produced over this period by T. Whitelegg until 1910 and thereafter by his son, R. H. Whitelegg.

The Midland Railway absorbed the LTSR in 1912, but although it placed the imprint of Derby on all the locomotives by removing the names which they had hitherto carried, and making other sundry minor alterations, the class continued to hold undisputed sway on the line. It was even perpetuated by the LMS, who constructed 35 further engines between 1923 and 1930.

There were, broadly speaking, three main varieties. The first lot, the smallest, consisted of 48 engines built between 1880 and 1898; these were Nos. 1 to 48 in the LTSR list. An enlarged version, the 'intermediates', appeared in 1900, Nos. 51–68. Between 1905 and 1911 the last twelve engines of the original class, Nos. 37–48, were rebuilt with much larger boilers. These constituted the basis of the final enlarged version, of which four new engines, Nos. 79–82, were turned out in 1909.

When taken over by the Midland in 1912, all lost their green livery and names in favour of the well-known crimson lake, and became MR Nos. 2110–2179. When the new LMS engines appeared in 1923 they took some of these numbers, and thereafter a certain amount of confusing renumbering took place. Briefly, the small class finished up as 2056–2091, and all were withdrawn between 1929 and 1936. The 'intermediate' class became 2092–2109; three of them lasted to become BR Nos. 41922, 41923, and 41925, but all had gone by 1953.

The largest class were finally 41953–41964 (the earlier LTSR built engines), and 41928–41952 and 41969–41978, the LMS ones, which had been originally 2110–2134 and 2151–2160. Four of these still remained in service in 1959. No. 80 *Thundersley* has been preserved in its old LTSR colours, and is to be seen at Bressingham Hall.

Sundry modifications appeared among the LTSR engines at various times. The earliest of the small class originally had stovepipe chimneys, and four were fitted with condensing apparatus. In later years some of them acquired extended smokeboxes, as did most of the intermediate ones and all of the

59

LT&SR *Thundersley*

larger ones, the latter also being superheated.

As the LTSR was a Westinghouse line, all engines necessarily had this brake, but many were dual-fitted for working other companies' stock over its lines.

Final dimensions as applied to 'Thundersley':
Driving wheels 6′ 6″   Cylinders 19″ × 26″   Pressure 170 lb

1882   Stroudley 0–4–2s

Stroudley's main line express locomotives for the London Brighton & South Coast Railway were unusual in that while other designers at this period were building engines mainly of the 2–4–0 or 4–4–0 types, the Brighton engines had no leading bogie or even pony truck.   The use of large front coupled wheels for express work was considered in some quarters to be somewhat hazardous, but the engines turned out to be very steady runners; there is no record of any of them having been derailed at speed. The design proved to be an excellent one, and these locomotives took their turns along with more modern classes on the principal Brighton expresses well into the present century.

The first engine was No. 214 *Gladstone*, completed in 1882, and 35 others followed up to 1891, Nos.

215–220 and 172–200. The last mentioned were built in reverse order, Nos. 198–200 in December 1887, 196 and 197 in May 1888, and so on, until the last one, No. 172 *Littlehampton* appeared in April 1891. The last ten came out after Stroudley's death in 1889. The class had been preceded by the six somewhat similar engines built in 1878–80, but with rather smaller dimensions these never achieved the success of the 'Gladstones', and they had all gone by 1904. Of the 'Gladstones' themselves, ten were scrapped prior to the First World War, but no more withdrawals took place until 1923.

The last to remain in traffic was No. B172, until 1932. *Gladstone* itself, on withdrawal in 1926, was restored to its original condition through the efforts of the Stephenson Locomotive Society, the first instance of preservation by a private organization in this country. As there was no suitable accommodation for it in the south, the question of housing was solved through the generosity of the LNER who agreed to it being placed in its own museum at York, where it has remained ever since. This museum is temporarily closed but is due to reopen in larger premises in 1975.

LB&SCR *Gladstone* at Clapham Junction in 1927 fully restored and en route to its final resting-place in York Museum

The engines were rebuilt by Marsh from 1906 onwards, and many of them acquired boilers with Ramsbottom safety valves over the firebox. The copper-capped chimneys in many cases gave way to plain cast iron ones, the yellow livery was replaced by Marsh's chocolate brown, and most of them lost their names. Under Southern auspices the colour was again changed to green, the numbers became B172, etc. (none ever received a 2000 number), and the few remaining names disappeared, including that of 184, which had borne the name of *Stroudley* in commemoration of its designer.

Dimensions:
Driving wheels 6' 6"   Cylinders $18\frac{1}{4}'' \times 26''$ Pressure 150 lb

1882   Adams 4–4–2Ts

71 of these engines were constructed by W. Adams for the London & South Western Railway between 1882 and 1885 for suburban work in the London area. The later engines of the class, built in 1884 and 1885, were slightly larger than the original 30 engines, their water capacity being increased from 1000 to 1200 gallons. The original series was completely devoid of side tanks, the water being carried partly in a well tank, and partly in the bunker below the coal. Even in the later engines only very small side tanks were provided over the rear driving wheels. Large numbers were taken out of service in 1916 when electrification of the LSWR suburban service began, but owing to war conditions they were not broken up and remained in Eastleigh yard in varying stages of decay for several years. One of them, No. 0488, was sold out of service, being later acquired by the East Kent Railway in 1919 as their No. 5.

By 1928 only two remained in possession of the Southern Railway, Nos. 0125 and 0520. These were specially retained for working the Lyme Regis branch, which has many sharp curves, and for which no other engines were found so suitable as these old-timers, with their flexible wheel bases. In course of time it was found that two engines were hardly adequate for maintaining the service; if one was away in shops, it left only one to carry on, with no spare in case of breakdown. Fortunately the East

LSWR Adams 4—4—2T No. 3488 as running in 1949

Kent engine was still in existence, and the Southern were able to buy it back in 1946; it returned to the fold under its original number, increased by 3000, as 3488 (0125 and 0520 having in the meantime become 3125 and 3520).

On nationalization in 1948 the three engines became BR 30582–30584 and continued to work the Lyme Regis branch until 1961, each in turn for a week at a time, the other two being kept in Exmouth Junction shed. The line was then taken over by the Western Region and subsequently closed. In consequence, all three were withdrawn in 1961, but fortunately No. 30583 was secured for preservation and can now be seen at work on the Bluebell Railway, restored to its old livery as LSWR 488.

Dimensions:
Driving wheels 5′ 7″   Cylinders 17½″ × 24″   Pressure 160 lb

1882   Steam Tram Engines

Steam locomotives for hauling tram-type coaches and other vehicles were used a good deal in urban areas, and in some towns themselves, notably London and the Midlands.   They were also used on some rural roadside systems during the later years of the 19th century, and in a few cases well into the 20th.   The last of all to remain operational was the Wisbech and Upwell, still steam worked until the 1950s, and latterly diesel, with final closure in 1966.   It had not, however, carried passengers since 1928.

The distinctive little engines for these lines were mostly built by Beyer, Peacock & Co., or Kitson & Co. which firms specialized in this field.   In all, four engines have survived for preservation, two Kitsons from the Portstewart Tramway in Northern Ireland, both in museums, one at Belfast and one at Hull, Yorkshire.   A Beyer, Peacock specimen built for the Rochdale & Oldham Steam Tramway is to be found at Dinting, at the premises of the Bahamas Loco Society.   There is another very interesting one which was ordered by the New South Wales Government and shipped to Australia in 1885, and which eventually came back to reappear at the maker's works at Manchester in 1890 for use as their shunting locomotive.   It has now been acquired by the Tramway Museum Society, Crich, Derbyshire, and can occasionally be seen in steam.

Engines of this type were almost invariably of the 0–4–0T wheel arrangement with shields protecting roadside traffic from the wheels and motion; usually the whole machine was totally enclosed over the boiler with a driver's cab at both ends.

Dimensions varied, but would be in the region of Driving wheels 2′ 6″   Cylinders $9\frac{1}{2}″ \times 12″$ Pressures about 150 lb

1883   Penrhyn and Dinorwic Railways, Hunslet 0–4–0STs

These little engines deserve a place in history, not only because they are worthy representations of a type of narrow gauge engine used in many places and locations, but also for the fact that so many of them have survived for preservation. The particular design in question consisted of a series of 35 engines, all built by the Hunslet Engine Co., Leeds, between 1883 and 1932, for use in the extensive slate quarries, among the largest in the world, at Bethesda and Llanberis in Caernarvonshire.

By the time that the quarries were abandoned in the 1960s the preservation movement had already attained considerable proportions and these locomotives, because of their small size and the comparatively easy prospects of transportation, were eagerly sought after by individuals, societies and preservation bodies. The result is that almost all of them have survived, a good many under private ownership and not on public view, while several have even gone to the USA and Canada.

Among those which are sometimes available for inspection, or even to be seen in steam may be mentioned the following:
Gwynneth at Bressingham Hall, Norfolk.
George Sholto at Bressingham Hall, Norfolk.
Elidir (formerly *Red Damsel*) on the Llanberis Lake

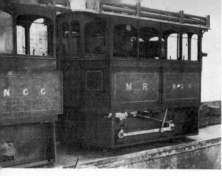

Former Portstewart Railway tram engine typical of its type, now restored and preserved in Belfast Museum

Gwynneth, quarry engine for the Penrhyn Railway

GWR Dean 0–6–0, on loan to War Department, 1942

Railway, open to tourism in the summer.
Dolbadarn on the Llanberis Lake Railway, open to tourism in the summer.
Irish Mail on West Lancashire Light Railway.
Rough Pup in the Narrow Gauge Museum, Towyn.
Hugh Napier in Penrhyn Castle Museum.
Elin on the Lincolnshire Coast Railway.
Holy War at Quainton Road, Bucks.
Cloister at the Hampshire Narrow Gauge Railway Society.

Although all basically of one class, there were differences in detail over the years, and the general dimensions can only be summarized on the average.

Driving wheels 1′ 8″   Cylinders 7″ × 20″   Weight 6¾ tons

The gauge of the Dinorwic Railway was 1′ 10¾″ and that of the Penrhyn 1′ 11½″.

The last mentioned had a main line to the coast, several miles in length (as did also the Dinorwic, with a gauge of 4′ 0″, see page 25).   It was worked by three somewhat larger, but very similar engines, *Charles, Blanche* and *Linda*.   The first mentioned is now in Penrhyn Castle Museum, and its two sisters, in somewhat rebuilt form and fitted with tenders, are on the Festiniog Railway, where they can be seen at work during the season.

1883   GWR Goods Engines

Dean's standard 0-6-0 for the GWR, of which 280 were built between 1883 and 1899, Nos. 2301–2580. Nos. 2361–2380 differed slightly from the others in having outside frames.   Many of them were taken over by the Government during both world wars for military service, mainly overseas; some never returned, but many did. In a few instances the same engine was 'called up' in both conflicts.

The illustration on page 66 shows one of them (No. 2529) as running under the War Department in 1942–4. The engine did duty at Bicester Ordnance Depot, near Oxford.

No. 2516 is now preserved in Swindon Museum.

General dimensions:
Driving wheels 5′ 2″ Cylinders 17½″ × 24″ Pressure 180 lb

North Eastern 'Tennant' 2–4–0 in York Museum

1885 NER Tennant 2–4–0s

A North Eastern design of express engine produced by a committee under the chairmanship of Henry Tennant, at that time the General Manager of the company. The original engine, No. 1463, which ran until 1927, has a permanent home in York Museum, due to be reopened in 1975.

Dimensions:
Driving wheels 7′ 1″ Cylinders 18″ × 24″ Pressure 140 lb

1886 Caledonian Railway Single Wheeler

This engine, the solitary example of its class, was constructed by Neilson & Co. in 1886 for the Edinburgh exhibition, at the end of which it was taken over by the Caledonian Railway. Although designed primarily by the makers, Dugald Drummond, then locomotive superintendent of the CR, evidently had a hand in it as it embodied certain of his characteristic features such as the cab and boiler

Caledonian Railway single wheeler No. 123

mountings. It was the only late 19th-century single wheeler to appear on a Scottish railway. It took part in the 1888 race to Scotland between the west and east coast routes, when it ran between Carlisle and Edinburgh with a load of four coaches, maintaining a daily average time of $107\frac{3}{4}$ minutes for the $100\frac{3}{4}$ miles. This included the ascent of Beattock bank, nine miles of continuous climbing between 1 in 74 and 1 in 88, preceded by a further three miles at 1 in 202.

For a number of years after the First World War

it was used only for hauling the directors' saloon trains, but in the early 1930s it was again put into ordinary traffic on local trains between Perth and Dundee. Meanwhile it had received a new boiler, with Ramsbottom safety valves over the firebox instead of mounted in the dome. It was withdrawn from service in 1935 and restored to its Caledonian blue livery for preservation, with its original number 123. This latter had earlier altered to 1123, and while in service with the LMS it was No. 14010. In 1957 it received a thorough overhaul before being put into working order for working enthusiasts' specials, which it did for a number of years. It was seen at times all over the country, even as far south as Sussex. It is now at rest in Glasgow Museum.

Dimensions:
Driving wheels 7′ 0″ Bogie wheels 3′ 6″ Cylinders 18″ × 26″ Pressure 160 lb

1887 Johnson's 4–2–2s

S. W. Johnson's magnificent single wheelers, sometimes nicknamed 'spinners', are considered by many to be the loveliest engines ever built. Their introduction in 1887 was something of a surprise, as the MR had built no single driving engines since 1866, but the invention of the steam sanding blast made single wheelers once more a practical proposition for the moderate loads of the day. The appearance of the Midland engine gave the single a new lease of life, if only temporary, and inside cylindered 4–2–2s began to appear also on the North Eastern, Great Western, Great Eastern, Great Northern and the Great Central railways. [It is doubtful whether a couple of Great Northern of Ireland engines built in 1885 or the Caledonian of 1886 (see page 69) had any influence on Johnson's design.]

Midland Railway Johnson single wheeler

No fewer than 95 of the Midland 4–2–2s appeared of five varieties, in which the dimensions were successively increased. The final ten, which came out in 1900, were considerably larger. The first of these was the well-known *Princess of Wales*, then numbered 2601 (later 685) and one of the only two Midland engines ever to bear a name. This class had the dome placed on the third ring of the boiler directly over the driving wheel, whereas on the earlier engines it had a more forward position on the second ring—a minor detail perhaps, but one which rather spoiled the balance of the design.

Appearance apart, however, these were magnificent engines, and very economical in operation with a load within their capacity. They proved themselves capable of handling up to ten bogies— about 300 tons, unassisted over the Midland main line south of Leicester. In later years they were used chiefly for piloting expresses or for hauling local stopping trains. During the First World War they were to be seen on the somewhat unsuitable task of piloting 0–6–0s on freight trains, or even on occasions a pair of them handling a heavy goods train themselves. The first engine, No. 25, later 600, was latterly fitted with a Deeley cab and kept exclusively for working the directors' saloon.

All remained in service until 1919, after which scrapping proceeded steadily, but several lasted into LMS days. The last lot, the 'Princesses', fared the worst, and were among the first to go, most of them being laid off by 1920; all had been broken up by 1922. The last engine in service was No. 673, and on withdrawal in 1928 it was repainted in MR colours with its old No. 118, and is happily preserved for posterity. It is at the time of writing at Stoneygate Museum, Leicester, but will eventually be moved to the new larger premises now planned.

Numbers after 1907
600–607, 610–619
Driving wheels 7′ 4½″ Cylinders 18″ × 26″ Pressure 160 lb
608, 609, 620–659
Driving wheels 7′ 6½″ Cylinders 18½″ × 26″ Pressure 160 lb
660–669
Driving wheels 7′ 6½″ Cylinders 19″ × 26″ Pressure 160 lb
670–684
Driving wheels 7′ 9½″ Cylinders 19½″ × 26″ Pressure 170 lb
685–694
Driving wheels 7′ 9½″ Cylinders 19½″ × 26″ Pressure 180 lb

1888   North British 0–6–0s

A standard design of 0–6–0 introduced by Matthew Holmes for general freight work on the NBR, typical of many of that period, of which one example survives.

168 of these engines were built between 1888 and 1900, and the class achieved some small degree of fame in that 25 of them served overseas during the First World War. All of them were returned and given commemorative names. The bestowing of such distinction on humble goods engines has

NBR 0–6–0, which saw service in France during the First World War

always been very rare on the main lines of Great Britain, although quite common at one time on the Midland Great Western and the Great Northern of Ireland. The preserved engine *Maude*, one of those which served abroad, originally NBR 673, built by Neilson & Co. in 1891, and eventually BR 65243, can be seen at the premises of the Scottish Railway Preservation Society at Falkirk.

Dimensions:
Driving wheels 5′ 0″ Cylinders 18¼″ × 26″ Pressure 165 lb

1888   Great North of Scotland 4–4–0s

The GNoSR was unique in that the only types of tender engine it ever employed were of the 2–4–0 and 4–4–0 pattern, both for passenger and goods work, for which it never adopted the almost universal 0–6–0.   The earlier engines had outside cylinders, but from 1888 onwards an inside cylinder design was introduced by Mr J. Manson which, with sundry variations, was to become standard with successive locomotive superintendents for the rest of the company's existence until 1923.

One of the ultimate version, built by Mr T. E. Heywood in 1920, No. 49 *Gordon Highlander*, which eventually became BR 62277, was restored in 1958 to its original state in working order as GNoSR No. 49, and used for several years on enthusiasts' specials. It is now in Glasgow Museum.

Dimensions
Driving wheels 6′ 1″   Cylinders 18″ × 26″   Pressure 165 lb

1889   Lancashire & Yorkshire Railway 2–4–2Ts

The L&YR was a very large user of this type. Designed by Mr J. A. F. Aspinall, 330 of them were built between 1889, when they first appeared, and 1911.   The general design was similar throughout the period, but underwent some minor modifications as time went on.   The engines were fitted with a special type of water pick-up apparatus which could operate in both directions, as it was frequently necessary to take up water when running bunker first.

These remarkable locomotives did a tremendous amount of hard work with heavy trains over the steeply graded lines of the L&YR; their duties were

GNoSR
*Gordon
Highlander*

L&YR Aspinall
2–4–2T

by no means confined to local services; they were regularly used as express engines on main line trains, along with much larger types of tender engines. At nationalization in 1948, 123 of them passed into BR hands. A handful was still in existence in 1959, and the original engine, No. 1008, has been restored to its L&YR livery for preservation. It can be seen at the Tyseley Steam Centre.

Dimensions:
Driving wheels 5′ 8″   Cylinders 18″ × 26″   Pressure 160 lb

LNWR Final design of 0–8–0

1889 0–8–0 Tender Engines

This type originated in this country on the comparatively small Barry Railway in South Wales. In 1886–8 Sharp, Stewart & Co. built 20 such engines for a railway in Sweden, but for some reason they were never delivered, possibly owing to payment not being forthcoming. In 1889 the Barry Railway bought two of them, and another two in 1897, when they were still on the maker's hands. Owing to the small turntables on the Barry system, which otherwise relied entirely on tank engines, they had to be fitted with four-wheeled tenders. They eventually became GWR Nos. 1387–1390, and they worked until the late 1920s.

In 1893 the type appeared on the LNWR; Mr Webb was still absorbed with his compounding, and he built 100 engines of this wheel arrangement with three cylinders, and another 170 with four cylinders between 1901 and 1905. As the subsequent history of these engines is a complicated one, it is sufficient to say that some of them were later rebuilt as simples by Mr George Whale, and some converted in the compound state to 2–8–0s. For the rest of its existence the LNWR relied on the 0–8–0 type as its standard for freight work, and from 1912 onwards some two or three hundred more were built, the last being a superheated version, the G2, introduced by Mr M. Beames in 1921.

The first of these, LNWR 485 and later LMS 9395, has been preserved by BR. Destined for exhibition in Leicester Museum, but not on view at the time of writing.

Dimensions:
Driving wheels 4′ 5½″   Cylinders 20½″ × 24″
Pressure 175 lb

Another large user of the 0–8–0 was the North Eastern, which it again adopted exclusively for its heavy mineral traffic. There were three classes, all of them following a general pattern with outside cylinders.

NER Large 3 cylinder 0–8–0

The earliest was Class T1 (LNER Q5), and 90 were built between 1901 and 1905, which eventually were allocated BR Nos. 63250–63339, although not all survived to carry these numbers. Class T2 (LNER Q6), 63340–63459, 110 engines between 1913 and 1920, and finally a large three cylinder version, T3 (LNER Q7), 15 engines, built in 1919–24, BR 63460–63474.

LSWR Adams 0–4–4T latterly used in the Isle of Wight

Two of these North Eastern engines have survived the first of the T3s, No. 63460, officially preserved by BR, but not at the moment of writing on public view, and one of the T2s, on the North Yorkshire Moors Railway, where it is in active use. This is BR 63395, at present restored under its LNER No. 3395, but it may eventually revert to its original North Eastern condition as 2238.

Other considerable users of the 0–8–0 type were the Lancashire & Yorkshire, Great Northern, and Great Central (the Hull & Barnsley also had a few).

In 1929 Sir Henry Fowler introduced it to the LMS, and an entirely new design evolved, but with strong Midland characteristics, and this could well be regarded as an MR 0–8–0 had that railway ever aspired to anything larger than a 0–6–0 for its mineral traffic. 175 of these were built. To complete this story of the 0–8–0 in this country it is only necessary to mention a few on the Caledonian and the solitary GER example mentioned on page 103.

1889   LSWR Adams 4′ 10″ 0–4–4Ts

Sixty of these useful little engines were built by William Adams at the Nine Elms works of the London & South Western Railway between 1889 and 1895, numbered 177–236.

They were widely used all over the system, chiefly on shunting duties and on branch lines.

After the grouping in 1923 they started to be drafted to the Isle of Wight to replace the somewhat miscellaneous lot of locomotives, some of them quite aged, which the Southern Railway inherited from the three independent lines on the island.

Eventually 23 of them found their way over there, being renumbered W14 to W36, and given names associated with the Isle of Wight. They were provided with larger bunkers to give increased coal capacity, but otherwise the only important change to the class as a whole was the substitution in some cases of Drummond boilers, with Ross 'pop' safety valves on the dome, which were not in general found to be an improvement. In addition the old Adams stove chimney was replaced by one of the Drummond pattern. During the last years of steam in the Isle of Wight this was the only class of engine to be found on the poor truncated remains of the island's rail system.

One of the last in service, No. 24 *Calbourne* (originally LSWR 209) was acquired by the Wight Locomotive Society, and can be seen at its premises at Haven Street, occasionally in steam.

Dimensions:
Driving wheels 4′ 10″   Cylinders 17½″ × 24″   Pressure 160 lb

1893   LSWR Adams 4–4–0s

Mr William Adams' last designs of 4–4–0s for the LSWR appeared during the years 1890–6. There were 60 engines in all, 30 with 7′ 0″ wheels, being mainly intended for the Bournemouth and Weymouth lines and the London end east of Salisbury, and 6′ 6″ for the more hilly routes to the west, a tradition which had grown up over the years.

All had been withdrawn from service by 1945, but by 1948 a few were still lying around at Eastleigh. Of these No. 563, built in 1893, was selected for preservation, and fully restored to its original condition. It was in Clapham Museum until its closure in 1973 and will reappear in due course at York or some other location.

Dimensions:
Driving wheels 6′ 7″   Cylinders 19″ × 26″   Pressure 175 lb

1893   NER Worsdell 4–4–0s

Mr Wilson Worsdell built several series of 4–4–0s for express working over the North Eastern Railway during the 1890s and 1900s, of which class M was typical.

Two of these engines, Nos. 1620 and 1621, of a batch of 20 built in 1893 (Nos. 1620–1639) achieved fame in the Race to Scotland of 1895 between the

LSWR
Adams
express
4–4–0
design

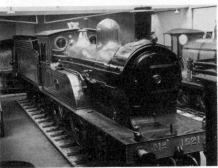

NER
Worsdell
4–4–0 in
York
Museum

east and west coast routes, on August 21/22 of that
year. With a train of six heavy joint stock coaches,
No. 1621 ran from York to Newcastle in $78\frac{1}{2}$
minutes at an average speed of 61·5 mph, and No.
1620 achieved a then world record by completing
the subsequent $124\frac{1}{2}$ miles to Edinburgh in 1 hr
53 min with an average speed of 66 mph. No. 1621,
which lasted until 1945, found an honoured place in
York Museum.

Dimensions:
Driving wheels 7′ 1″   Cylinders 19″ × 26″   Pressure
160 lb

1894 Highland Railway Jones Goods

These engines are notable as being the first example of the 4–6–0 type in the British Isles, a wheel arrangement destined to become very widely used on nearly all main lines in subsequent years. The 15 pioneer engines on the HR were built by Sharp, Stewart & Co. in 1894, and were at the time the most powerful main line engines in the country. Originally intended principally as freight engines, they were often called upon for passenger duties during the wide fluctuations of traffic which occurred on the Highland Railway, particularly during the summer season. As HR Nos. 103–117, they duly became LMS Nos. 17916–17930 and did a great deal of hard work before being gradually taken out of service between 1929 and 1940.

Fortunately the original engine was set aside for preservation, repainted at first in HR light green, but after the war in the short-lived—so far as the HR was concerned—Stroudley's 'improved engine green', which was in fact a brilliant yellow. In

Highland Railway. The first 4–6–0 in the British Isles

1959 it was put back in working order and ran many enthusiasts' trains for several years before finding a permanent resting-place in Glasgow Museum.

It is the only Highland engine to have survived, although a Drummond 4–4–0 *Ben Alder* was retained for many years with this object in view before unaccountably being dispatched to the scrap-breakers in 1966.

Dimensions:
Driving wheels 5′ 3″   Cylinders 20″ × 28″   Pressure 175 lb

1895 Snowdon Mountain Rack Rail Locomotives

The only rack rail mountain railway in the British Isles is up Snowdon in North Wales, although such systems are found in considerable numbers in other parts of Europe, notably in Switzerland.   These are now nearly all electrically worked, but Snowdon remains one of the last bastions of commercially run railways in this country that is still steam operated. With a gradient of 1 in 5½, special locomotives incorporating a rack and pinion system have to be used.   This consists of a double steel rack between the 2′ 7½″ gauge running rails, which engages the teeth of the two geared cogwheels on the engine. The teeth of each rack are staggered so that at least three of them are in gear at any one time.   The locomotives, which always face up the mountain and have the coach at the upper end as a precaution against a runaway, have inclined boilers which procure an approximately horizontal position when the engine is on the gradient.   All were supplied by the Swiss Locomotive Co. and are 0–4–2Ts of two varieties.   The first five, built in 1895/6 were Nos. 1 *Ladas*, 2 *Enid*, 3 *Wyddfa*, 4 *Snowdon*, and 5 *Moel*

Snowdon Mountain Railway rack locomotive

Siabod, and were followed by an improved version in 1922/3 by Nos. 6 *Padarn*, 7 *Aylwin* and 8 *Eryri*. No. 1 had a very short life as it was blown over the mountainside in a gale in 1896 and never recovered, but the others are all still in active service during the summer season.

Dimensions:
Driving wheels 2′ 1¾″   Cylinders 11¾″ × 23¾″
Rack pinions 1′ 10¼″ diameter   Pressure 200 lb

1896   McIntosh Caledonian Engines

No account of the general history of British steam locomotive development can be written without brief reference to engines of the Caledonian Railway around the turn of the century, although no specimens have survived for preservation.

Mr J. F. McIntosh became locomotive superintendent of the CR in 1895, and inaugurated what became known as the 'big engine' policy, later to be followed by many other railways. His *Dunalastair*

4–4–0s were of four varieties, the first of which appeared in 1896, with successive enlargements in 1897, 1899 and 1904, all of which were known as Dunalastair I, II, III and IV respectively. His successor in 1914, Mr W. Pickersgill, continued with the same basic design, and construction was continued to the last years before the grouping in 1922. The last of them was withdrawn in 1961 and there were hopes for its preservation, but this unfortunately did not materialize. Best known of all was McIntosh's No. 903 *Cardean*, one of his inside cylinder 4–6–0s, built in 1903 and 1906, seven engines in all, Nos. 49 and 50, and 903–907. No. 907 was involved in the Quintinhill disaster of 1915, the worst in British railway history, and was scrapped in consequence. The others lasted until 1927–33. *Cardean* achieved a somewhat unique record in working the same train for ten years, except of course when undergoing servicing or repairs, the 2.0 pm 'Corridor' from Glasgow to Carlisle, returning with the corresponding train from London.

Dimensions:
Driving wheels 6′ 6″   Cylinders 20″ × 26″   Pressure 200 lb (175 lb after superheating)

Cardean a well-known CR McIntosh locomotive

1897 Glasgow & South Western Railway 4 cylinder 4–4–0

1897 was the year in which 4 cylinder locomotives first appeared in this country (apart from articulated engines such as the Festiniog 'Fairlies') and three railways introduced them almost simultaneously: the Glasgow & South Western, the London & North Western and the London & South Western. The G&SWR engine built by James Manson was first in the field; it employed simple propulsion through the four cylinders which were situated in line with the smokebox. The inside cylinders had a common steam chest between them, the valves being worked by Stephenson's link motion, which through rocking shafts also operated the valves of the outside cylinders. The engine ran in this form until 1923 when Whitelegg rebuilt it with piston valves and a very large boiler. Originally No. 11, it had been renumbered 394 in 1919 and on rebuilding it acquired a name, *Lord Glenarthur*, the only G&SWR engine to do so. It became LMS No. 14509 and was scrapped in 1934.

Brief reference should here be made to the fact that two months after the appearance of the G&SWR engine, Mr F. W. Webb built two 4 cylinder 4–4–0's, one of which was a compound. This engine, No. 1502 *Black Prince*, differed from his previous efforts in compound propulsion (see page 47) in that the driving wheels were coupled and also that together with its sister No. 1501 *Jubilee*, these were the first LNWR engines to have a leading bogie.

In the same year Mr Dugald Drummond introduced on the LSWR a somewhat similar engine, in this case a sort of hybrid in that although it had 4 cylinders the driving wheels were uncoupled (as in the earlier Webb compounds); in this case the two

Britain's first 4 cylinder main line locomotive, G&SWR
No. 11

inside cylinders drove the front wheels, the outside
ones the rear. As such it was a 4–2–2–0 and not a
4–4–0. Although five more were built, which
lasted for many years, they were not used a great
deal and the design cannot be regarded as a success.
Neither can the two others just referred to, but they
form an important link in the history of the express
passenger engine. Needless to say, none has
survived for preservation.

1897

Dean's inside cylinder outside framed 4–4–0s must
take a place in locomotive history if only for the fact
that the original design, which originated in 1897,
and continued with modification until 1908
included the famous *City of Truro*. This achieved
history in being the first steam locomotive to attain
an authenticated speed of 100 mph. (Although the
actual figure of 102·3 mph has been latterly dis-
puted, it was undoubtedly a world record at the
time and as near enough to the round figure to
make any real difference.)

City of Truro itself was one of a batch of ten
engines which came out in 1903, and it ran until
1931, when it was withdrawn from service and

placed in York Museum. In 1957 it was resuscitated and restored to working order, mainly for the running of enthusiasts' specials. This was an admirable enterprise that was shortly followed by the Scottish Region, and happily pursued for a few years in other parts of the country until the hierarchy of British Railways imposed an absolute clamp down when general steam operation finally ceased in 1968.

City of Truro is now safely ensconced in Swindon Museum, where it can be inspected, but for the time being at any rate it is unlikely to be seen in steam again.

Principal dimensions (as finally running)
Driving wheels 6′ 8½″ Cylinders 18″ × 26″ Pressure 200 lb

1898 North Eastern Railway 0–6–0Ts Class J72

This remarkable little design is unique in that it was constructed over a period of 53 years, under three different stages of railway ownership and during five régimes of locomotive superintendents.

The design was that of William Worsdell, whose period of office on the old North Eastern Railway ran from 1890 to 1910. The first 20 engines were built at Darlington in 1898 and 1899, but no more

GWR, the speed record-breaking *City of Truro* as restored and running in 1957

appeared until 1914, by which time Sir Vincent Raven was in charge; then 20 more were built, with very slight modifications to the original design. Others followed, ten in 1920 and another 25 in 1922. After the grouping Gresley built another ten at Doncaster in 1925, bringing the total up to 85. This might have been considered the end of the story, but after nationalization British Railways ordered yet another 28. These were turned out under the superintendency of Peppercorn, who had succeeded Thompson on the LNER in 1946 and was the first CME of the Eastern and North Eastern Regions of British Railways.

These latest engines were again practically similar in every respect to the original design, and did not even embody such modern practices as the employment of the 'pop' safety valves, as might have been expected.

The North Eastern and LNER-built engines became BR Nos. 68670–68754 at nationalization, and as no provision had been made for further construction the new batch had to be numbered in a special series and came out as Nos. 69001–69028.

All remained in service until 1958, when some of the earlier engines began to be withdrawn from traffic.

It is perhaps unfortunate that none of the original NER engines survived for preservation, but one of the post-nationalization ones has been acquired on behalf of the Keighley & Worth Valley Railway, and can now be seen, sometimes in steam, at Haworth or Oxenhope. It retains its BR number 69023, but has been repainted in NER livery and named *Joem*.

Dimensions:
Driving wheels 4' 1¼″ Cylinders 17″ × 24″ Pressure 140 lb

LNER J72
class 0–6–0T

Britain's first 'atlantic' engine, GNR *Henry Oakley*

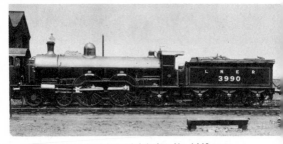

The enlarged GNR 'atlantic' design, No. 1442, was
for many years the engine allocated for working royal
trains

The term 'atlantic', generally applied to the 4–4–2 tender engine, is thought to have been derived from the fact that although it had been used in America for a number of years, it was not until 1898 that it crossed the ocean and first appeared in this country. It was introduced by Mr H. A. Ivatt, on the Great Northern, the first engine being No. 990. It achieved the remarkable distinction for the Great Northern in bearing a name, *Henry Oakley*, after the Company's General Manager, the only example in the whole of its history until the appearance of the pacific *Great Northern* right at the end of its individual existence in 1922 (see page 134). 22 of the class were constructed and were followed in 1902 by a considerably enlarged version. The main difference was a much larger boiler and a wide firebox of maximum width extending over the frame, that was made possible by the small trailing wheels beneath. A total of 94 of this type were built up to the year 1910, and these worked the whole of the principal main line expresses until the coming of the pacifics already mentioned. There were one or two miscellaneous variations, including two built as 4 cylinder compounds but subsequently converted to simple. The first engines of both main classes, the original 990 and the prototype 251 of the larger variety, have survived, in York Museum, and were steamed in the 1950s for working a few enthusiasts' specials.

In 1899 the Lancashire & Yorkshire was the second railway to adopt the atlantic. These were striking machines with 7′ 3″ driving wheels and, most unusually for the type, inside cylinders, and they earned the nickname 'Highflyers'. Some of them were fitted with a patent steam drier, an early form of superheater. In 1906 this was adopted, again on the L&YR, in an improved version designed by Herr W. Schmidt in Germany, and was soon to be followed by many other similar patterns and to become standard equipment for main line locomotives on all railways.

The 'atlantic' type was later adopted by the Great Western, Great Central, North Eastern, North British, and LB&SCR, the last named engines being almost identical with the large GNR type, as their designer, D. Earle Marsh, had come from Doncaster. From a post grouping angle, it is interesting that the atlantic was essentially the

L&YR 'Highflyer' atlantic

province of the LNER, in that four out of its six principal constituents used the type, and it was possible at one time to travel from London to Aberdeen behind examples from three different railways.

The NBR engines had extremely large boilers and were most impressive machines. The last one to run, No. 875, *Midlothian*, was set aside in 1939 for preservation, but owing to the onset of war it was regrettably broken up.

The Great Northern atlantic had 6′ 8″ driving wheels, with 170 lb pressure, with cylinders 19″ × 24″ in the smaller version and 20″ × 26″ in the larger; the latter, with increased heating surface, were much more powerful and considerably heavier.

The last NBR 'atlantic' *Midlothian*

1899 London & South Western Drummond 4–4–0s

Mr Dugald Drummond designed several classes of 4–4–0 for the LSWR, but the most successful of all were undoubtedly his early T9s of 1899. 66 of them came out within the space of three years, and they were never really eclipsed by his subsequent larger designs, still less by his somewhat unfortunate 4–6–0s. Even after the latter appeared the old T9s, which earned the nickname of 'greyhounds', were as often as not to be found on the expresses over the heavily graded line between Salisbury and Exeter in preference to the larger engines which should have replaced them.

In 1924 Mr Urie started fitting them with super-heaters, and in this form they were found to be even better machines. All were consequently fitted in

Drummond T9 class 4–4–0 No. 119, another engine specially maintained in tip-top condition for working royal trains. (See page 90)

this way. For many years No. 119 was the official engine for Royal trains, and it was kept in spick and span condition. Some engines of this type survived to the early 1960s; No. 120 has been preserved, repainted in LSWR Colours, and is at present on loan to the Standard Gauge Steam Trust, Tyseley.

Dimensions:
Driving wheels 6′ 7″   Cylinders 19″ × 26″   Pressure 175 lb

1900   GER Claud Hamiltons

The first engine of this famous class was designed by Mr James Holden, built at Stratford and numbered after the year of its birth, 1900. Subsequent engines were built in batches of ten and numbered successively backwards, 1890–1899, 1880–1889, and so on, until the final lot, which came out after the grouping under Gresley's régime, were LNER 1780E–1789E.

In their original state the 'Claud Hamiltons' with their well-proportioned outlines in the livery of the Great Eastern royal blue (a far richer colour than the present BR shade), embellished with elaborate lining out in red and gold, and a certain amount of decorative brasswork, were considered by many to be one of the most handsome designs ever built. Unfortunately in later years Gresley ruined their appearance by completely rebuilding many of them, and by the substitution of a new design of chimney in place of the shapely GER copper-capped ones, which did not suit them at all.

They were very efficient engines and did fine work on the tightly timed heavy expresses over a none too easy road. All lasted until nationalization days as

GER *Claud Hamilton*

BR 62500–62620, but they disappeared during the 1950s and regrettably none survived for preservation. There is however a fine large scale model of *Claud Hamilton* in the British Railway collection, until recently on view in Clapham Museum.

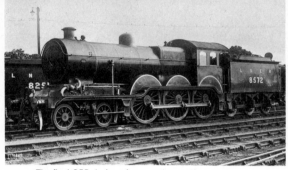
The final GER design of express locomotive

Their successors in GER days were some very similar and almost equally handsome 4–6–0s, with inside cylinders which were unusual for this type. These again were perpetuated as late as 1928 by Sir Nigel Gresley, when a final batch of ten appeared; one of these, No. 8572, has survived on the North Norfolk Preservation Society at Sheringham.

Dimensions:
Clauds as originally built
Driving wheels 7′ 0″   Cylinders 19″ × 26″   Pressure 185 lb
4–6–0s
Driving wheels 6′ 6″   Cylinders 20″ × 28″   Pressure 180 lb

1900   South Eastern & Chatham Railway

On the amalgamation of the old South Eastern and the London Chatham & Dover Railways in 1899 a new locomotive superintendent was appointed, Mr H. S. Wainwright. He introduced fresh designs of simple, robust and straightforward conventional types. The first of these consisted of a 4–4–0 for express passenger work; these initially came out in 1901, a 0–6–0, introduced in 1900 for freight and miscellaneous duties, and a 0–4–4T in 1904 for suburban services.

The last two were of rather plain appearance, although embellished by an elaborate lined out dark green livery and polished brass domes. The 4–4–0s had, however, decorated splashers surrounded by brass beading, and with their near perfect outline could rightly take their place among the most handsome engines ever designed. In all, 106 of the 0–6–0s were built, 63 of the 0–4–4Ts, and 50 of the 4–4–0s. 20 of the latter were later superheated and modernized by Mr Maunsell, but the remainder, and all of the other two classes, were virtually unchanged through their long working days, most lasting into the 1950s and some the early 1960s. All did yeoman service over the busy and difficult lines of the SE&CR throughout their careers. Fortunately, representatives of all three of these earlier classes have been preserved.

No. 737, one of the D class 4–4–0s just described, was preserved officially by BR and was on view in

SE&CR Wainright's handsome D class express 4–4–0

Clapham Museum until closure in 1973, and will probably in due course reappear at York. The other two classes are represented by C class 0–6–0 No. 592, to be found on the Bluebell Railway, and H class 0–4–4T No. 263 at Ashford steam centre. Both of these, which have been preserved privately, are in working order, and all three are fully restored to original condition.

SE&CR Wainwright's sturdy 0–6–0 design

Principal dimensions:

4–4–0 Class D Driving wheels 6′ 8″ Cylinders 19″ × 26″ Pressure 175 lb

0–6–0 Class C Driving wheels 5′ 2″ Cylinders 18½″ × 26″ Pressure 160 lb

0–4–4T Class H Driving wheels 5′ 6″ Cylinders 18″ × 26″ Pressure 160 lb

These well-known engines, regarded by many as being the only really successful compound design ever to work in this country, were introduced by Mr S. W. Johnson toward the end of his long and worthy career as Chief Mechanical Engineer of the Midland Railway, a position he held from 1873 until 1903.

Experiments in compounding had been tried by several railways during the latter part of the 19th century, notably by Mr Webb on the LNWR, with somewhat indifferent results, as already described in an earlier section.

Mr Johnson had been particularly impressed by an engine on the North Eastern Railway which had been built by Mr T. W. Worsdell on the two cylinder von Borries' system and which had also achieved a certain measure of success on various railways. It was rebuilt in 1898 with some entirely novel ideas, patented by Mr William Smith, at that time locomotive draughtsman on the NER.   These involved the use of three cylinders, two low pressure outside and one high pressure between the frames, and enabled the engine to be worked either as a compound, a semi-compound or as a simple.   By the use of a second regulator live steam could be admitted into all three cylinders, an immense advantage in starting a heavy train.   An intermediate stage between full simple and compound working could be obtained through a reducing valve which the driver could adjust to vary the pressure in the low-pressure steam chest.   This method of semi-compound working also proved invaluable in working a heavy train over a steep gradient or under other adverse conditions. Although no others like No. 1619 appeared on the North Eastern, Mr Johnson undoubtedly based his new engines on this design of which the initial five, Nos. 2631–2635, put up some fine work on the mountainous Settle–Carlisle line. Mr R. M. Deeley, who had succeeded Johnson, decided to build more engines of the same general design but with important differences. The chief difference was the provision of a patent regulator by which the engine always started non-compound and automatically changed over to full compound with the advance of the regulator. There were also some differences in external appearance, the running plate being raised clear of the coupling rods, while the rectangular rear splasher gave way to a quarter-circle blended into the cab side sheets.

30 of the new Deeley engines appeared in 1905–6, numbered 1000–1029. At the 1907 renumbering the original five Johnson engines took the numbers 1000–1004 and the Deeleys were increased by five, becoming 1005–1034. A further ten engines Nos. 1035–1044, came out in 1908–9.

No more were built in Midland days, but the design with slight modifications was adopted as a standard type early in the grouping, and no fewer than 195 further engines were turned out between 1924 and 1932, numbered 1045–1199 and 900–939. Still more were to have been constructed, but the order was cancelled when W. A. (later Sir William) Stanier appeared on the scene, as he had very different ideas on the subject of locomotive power.

Nos. 1000–1004 were eventually rebuilt in line with the Deeley engines, and at the same time were superheated: Nos. 1000 and 1004 in 1914, 1001 and 1003 in 1915, and 1002 in 1919. No. 1040 had already received a superheater in 1913, but it was not until 1919 that it was decided to superheat the remainder of the class commencing with No. 1009. The LMS-built engines were, of course, superheated from the start. These had 6′ 9″ driving wheels in place of the 7′ 0″ wheel on the original Midland engines.

The class as a whole did magnificent work. Possibly the greatest achievements were on the Caledonian and G&SW main lines in the immediate post grouping years. They also did remarkably well on the LNWR Birmingham two-hour expresses, but were possibly not quite so happy on the other LNWR main lines owing to an instinctive distrust of compounds by North Western men inherited from the Webb days. No. 1054 made history by running non-stop from Euston to Edinburgh, a distance of nearly 400 miles, in May 1928. This was the quiet answer of the LMS to

The original Midland compound as now restored and preserved

the LNER's announcement that it would run the *Flying Scotsman* non-stop between the two capital cities by the use of a corridor tender whereby the crew could be changed en route. The LMS reply to this was to divide the *Royal Scot* into two portions, one running non-stop to Glasgow and the other to Edinburgh. The performance was not repeated, but it effectively stole the limelight from the LNER performance.

With the decline in maintenance standards which set in during the Second World War the compounds gradually fell into some disrepute, as they required more attention in this respect than they received. Moreover they were largely put to work on local trains, duties for which they were unsuitable, and in consequence got a poor reputation through no fault of their own, as they were magnificent engines when kept in proper trim and well handled.

The beginning of the end was inevitable. All passed into BR hands at nationalization in 1948. No. 1002 was scrapped shortly afterwards in the same year, and all of the Midland ones had been withdrawn by 1952. A start was made on the LMS batch in 1953, and by the end of 1959 less than a dozen remained.

The original No. 41000 was fortunately kept in store at Crewe for a number of years, and in 1959 was fully restored to its rebuilt 1914 condition in Midland colours for preservation and for working special trains. It was later put on exhibition in Clapham Museum until closure in 1973 and will no doubt reappear in due course, possibly once more as a working engine in view of its excellent condition.

Dimensions:
Driving wheels 7′ 0″ Cylinders 1HP 19″ × 26″
2LP 21″ × 26″ Pressure 200 lb

1902 Great Eastern Railway 'Decapod'

This startling engine was built in 1902 to the designs of J. Holden and was totally unlike anything else which had appeared previously on the GER or any other line. It was indeed believed to be the most powerful locomotive in the world at the time.

The Great Eastern 'decapod'

No. 20 had an enormous boiler with a firebox extending the full width of the frame (as on the GNR atlantics of the same year) and the water was carried in a well tank beneath the bunker. It was the first ten-coupled engine in this country, and apart from two very early machines of 1846 and 1868 it was the first to be fitted with three simple propulsion cylinders. The middle pair of driving wheels was flangeless. Its purpose was purely experimental, to ascertain whether steam haulage was capable of attaining as great a rate of acceleration as electric traction for suburban working. The electrification advocates maintained that they could produce a train of 315 tons which could be accelerated to 30 mph in thirty seconds. The new engine, with a train of 335 tons, actually exceeded this target on test; as a result the question of electrifying the Great Eastern suburban lines was shelved for another decade. Unfortunately the necessary strengthening of track and bridges to take such heavy engines was also postponed on account of cost, and was in fact never carried out. Owing to the permanent way restrictions, the 'decapod' was never able to be used in ordinary service, and in 1906 was reconstructed as a 2 cylinder 0–8–0 tender engine with a smaller boiler, and was used on freight trains. It was finally scrapped in 1913. It was unfortunate that the engine was so much before its time and never had the opportunity of completely justifying itself.

Principal dimensions as 0–10–0T
Driving wheels 4′ 6″ Cylinders (3) $18\frac{1}{2}″ \times 24″$
Pressure 200 lb Weight 80 tons

The later story of the GER London lines, which in 1922 introduced the most intensive steam-operated suburban service in the world, can be conveniently dealt with here. This remarkable achievement, at first relying almost entirely on somewhat small engines of 0–4–4T, 0–6–0T and 2–4–2Ts types (of which one of the 0–6–0Ts, No. 87, was preserved in Clapham Museum until its closure, and is now due to be transferred to York) led to the construction of large numbers of somewhat more powerful engines

Typical engines of the final era of GER steam, Liverpool Street in 1957

of the 0–6–2Ts of a type originally introduced by Mr A. J. Hill in 1914. Sir Nigel Gresley, who became Chief Mechanical Engineer of the newly formed LNER in 1923 was a broad-minded man, and he continued construction of this very satisfactory type in large numbers although it was not his own design. These engines worked the bulk of the busy suburban service until this finally succumbed to electrification, inaugurated in 1949 and completed in 1960. One of them, built in 1924 as LNER 999E, later 7999 and ultimately BR 69621, has been preserved and is now at the premises of the Stour Valley Society, Chappell and Wakes Colne, Essex. The illustration, taken in 1957 shows one of the engines at Liverpool Street, together with one of the 0–6–0T class already referred to.

Principal dimensions:
Driving wheels 4' 10" Cylinders 18" × 24" Pressure 180 lb

1902   Vale of Rheidol Railway

This 1' 11½" Gauge line from Aberystwyth to Devil's Bridge in Wales is the only part of the British Railways nationalized system still operated by steam traction. Two 2–6–2Ts were built in 1902 by Davies & Metcalfe, No. 1 *Edward VII* and 2 *Prince of Wales*. In 1913 they were taken over by the Cambrian Railways and afterwards passed into the hands of the Great Western, where they became Nos. 1212/13. (They had lost their names by 1915.) Two further identical engines were built at Swindon in 1923, Nos. 7 and 8 in the GWR list. Of the originals, No. 1212 was scrapped in 1934, but the second engine, now numbered 9, has had its name *Prince of Wales* restored, while Nos. 7 and 8 are now known as *Owain Glyndŵr* and *Llewelyn*.

Vale of Rheidol narrow gauge 2–6–2T

They can now be seen actively at work during the summer season when the line is in operation, and have achieved the distinction of being the only steam engines now employed by BR and of having the standard blue livery.

Dimensions:
Driving wheels 2′ 6″ Cylinders $11\frac{1}{2}″ × 17″$ Pressure 165 lb

1902

The long and honoured history of the Great Western express passenger 4–6–0 dates from 1902 with the appearance of No. 100 *William Dean* (later No. 2900). This had a somewhat revolutionary appearance for the time and was destined to be the forerunner of one of the most successful series of engines in this country. This evolved into the 'Saint' class, which finally totalled 77 engines. Some were originally built as 'atlantics' but were later converted to 4–6–0s. Unfortunately none has survived. These were all two cylinder machines but No. 40 *North Star*, which later became No. 4000 and which appeared in 1906, had four cylinders, and

106

the ultimate class of 73 engines became known generally as the 'Star' class. No. 4003 *Lode Star* has been preserved and can be seen in Swindon Museum.

Possibly the most famous of all were the 'Castles', which followed from 1923 onwards, ultimately totalling 165 engines (plus a few more rebuilt from 'Stars'); the last of these did not appear until 1950 after the formation of British Railways. The original 4073 *Caerphilly Castle* has found an honoured place in the Science Museum, Kensington, and several others have been preserved in working order, such as 4079 *Pendennis Castle*, owned privately and not on general public view. 5051 *Earl Bathurst* is at the GWR Society's premises at Didcot, 7029 *Clun Castle* at the Standard Gauge Steam Trust, Tyseley, and there is the possibility of others from Barry scrapyard.

The ultimate development of the GWR 4 cylinder 4–6–0 was the 'King' class, introduced in 1927, and at the time the most powerful engine in the country.

The original No. 6000 *King George V*, which visited the United States soon after construction, is too well known to need further reference here beyond the fact that it is preserved at Bulmer's Cider

The original GWR 4–6–0 design of express engine No. 100 (later named *William Dean*)

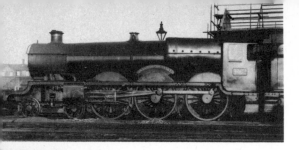

(*top*) A well-known engine of the class, No. 4082 *Windsor Castle*

(*centre*) The ultimate development of GWR 4–6–0 design, the 'King' class of 1927. No. 6003 *King George IV*

(*below*) GWR 2–8–0 freight engine

Factory, Hereford, and is sometimes to be found working enthusiasts' specials over BR main lines.

Another of the class, No. 6024 *King Edward I*, is to be found at Quainton Road, awaiting restoration.

1903

The Great Western was the first railway to introduce the two cylinder 2–8–0 heavy mineral engine to the British Isles, a type which eventually became much used by other lines, although it was to be some years before the example was followed by the Great Central, Great Northern, Somerset & Dorset, the LMS, the War Department in both world wars, and eventually British Railways.

In a way it could be said that the GWR engine was before its time. It is interesting to note that although the eventual total was 167 engines, Nos. 2800–2899 and 3800–3866, their construction was spread over an interval of 40 years, the last not appearing until 1942 (with a few small detail modifications from the original) and with a complete gap between 1919 and 1938.

No. 2818 has been preserved by the Bristol Corporation, although not available for public inspection. No. 2857 may be acquired by the Severn Valley Railway and there are other possibilities from Barry scrapyard.

General dimensions:
Driving wheels 4′ 7½″   Cylinders 18″ × 30″   Boiler pressure 225 lb

The year 1903 also saw the first 2–6–2Ts on the Great Western, a type which was to be much favoured by that railway for different categories of shorter distance passenger work, with variations in size according to the duties for which they were

GWR Branch line and cross country type of 2–6–2T

intended.   The most noticeable differences were in the size of the driving wheels, ranging from 5′ 8″ for more express work, 4′ 7½″ for branches and cross country lines, and a few 4′ 1½″ for exceptionally hilly routes.

Examples of the first two of these categories have survived.   The larger is represented by No. 6106, one of a modernized version built in 1931 for the London suburban services, and now to be seen in working order at the GWR Society's premises at Didcot.   There is also an earlier example, No. 5164, on the Severn Valley Railway.   Others are in negotiation from Barry scrapyard.

Of the intermediate class, No. 4555 and 4588 are to be often seen hard at work on the Dart Valley Railway, and its associated Torbay line, No. 5572 is at Taunton, 4566 on the Severn Valley and 5541 has been acquired by the Dean Forest Preservation Society.

1903 Welshpool & Llanfair Railway

Two 0–6–0Ts were built for the 2′ 6″ gauge Welshpool & Llanfair Railway by Beyer, Peacock & Co. in 1903, No. 1 *The Earl*, and No. 2 *The Countess*. They were later taken over by the Cambrian Railways and by the GWR at the grouping when they became Nos. 822/3, eventually passing into the hands of British Railways.

No passenger trains had been worked since 1931, but freight continued until 1956, when the line closed. Part of this line has now been reopened by the Welshpool & Llanfair Light Railway Preservation Company Limited, using among other locomotives the two original W&LR engines which had been placed in store with the project in view.

Dimensions:
Driving wheels 2′ 9″ Cylinders 11½″ × 16″ Pressure 150 lb

Welshpool & Llanfair narrow gauge 0–6–0T

(*upper*) L&LSR 4–8–0

(*lower*) L&LSR 4–8–4T

1905 Londonderry & Lough Swilly Railway 8 coupled engines

This 3′ 0″ gauge railway in the north-west of Ireland deserves mention by virtue of the fact that it had two designs of wheel arrangement never seen elsewhere in the British Isles, although there were only two examples of each. The first was a 4–8–0 tender engine of which two, Nos. 11 and 12, came from the works of Hudswell Clarke in 1905; these were supplemented in 1912 by two 4–8–4Ts, Nos. 5 and 6, from the same makers. They were very large engines indeed for the narrow gauge, in fact almost of comparable proportions to what might have been found on the standard gauge. They were designed to work over the tenuous 74-mile long line of the Letterkenny and Burtonport Extension Railway from Londonderry through the wildest parts of Donegal to the small seaport of Burtonport. No. 11 was scrapped in 1933, but the other lasted until the complete closure of the railway in 1953; it is unfortunate that none survived for preservation.

As already stated, they remained unique in design in the whole of the British Isles, although a 4–8–0 tender design was prepared for use on the Southern Railway, but was never built.

Principal dimensions:

	4–8–0	4–8–4T
Driving wheels	3′ 9″	3′ 9″
Cylinders	$15\frac{1}{2}″ \times 22″$	$16″ \times 20″$
Pressure	170 lb	180 lb

1908 Paget 2–6–2

This was an experimental engine constructed at Derby in 1908 to the design of the General Superintendent Cecil Paget, although R. M. Deeley was locomotive superintendent at the time.

There were eight cylinders, $18″ \times 12″$, in two groups of four, placed between the first and second, and the second and third driving axles. The middle axle had inside cranks, two driven by the pistons of the front group of cylinders and two by the rear ones. The fore and aft coupled axles each had two cranks, driven by the remaining two cylinders of the adjacent group. The movements of pistons and cranks were arranged so that all were balanced. The valves were of the sleeve type. It was incidentally the only 2–6–2 tender engine to run in this country until the appearance of *Green Arrow* on the LNER (see page 161).

The engine ran only a few trial trips, much leakage trouble being experienced with the sleeve valves. When it did get going it was said to be very fast and powerful, and attained 82 mph on test on one occasion. However, the authorities apparently soon lost interest in it, and for a long time it remained in Derby works covered by sheeting and no visitor was permitted near it. It was quietly cut up in 1919.

For many years no details or drawings of the engine or of its trials were allowed to be published, and No. 2299, as it was numbered, remained a sort of legendary myth to the railway enthusiasts of those days. It was not until after the grouping that details were finally available and the official photograph released for publication. Until that time very few people had more than the vaguest idea of what the engine had looked like, and some even expressed doubts as to whether it had ever existed. The official view of the engine is the only known photograph of it in existence.

Dimensions:
Driving wheels 5′ 4″   Leading and trailing wheels 3′ 3½″   Pressure 180 lb   Weight (approx) 77 tons

1908   GWR 'The Great Bear'

In 1908 there appeared the first and for many years the only 4–6–2 'pacific' engine to run in this country, the famous Great Western No. 111 *The Great Bear*. It was the most powerful express engine in Britain in its day, but owing to its weight it had to be restricted to the main line between

London and Bristol. For this reason it was never multiplied on the GWR to the end of that railway's existence, although the type was later used extensively on the LMS, LNER, and SR. In 1924 it was rebuilt as a 4–6–0 in conformity with the 'Castle' class and renamed *Viscount Churchill*, in which form it lasted until 1953.

Dimensions:
Driving wheels 6′ 8½″ Cylinders (4) 15″ × 26″
Pressure 225 lb

(*above*) The only known photograph of the secret and mysterious Paget engine of the Midland Railway

(*below*) The GWR's only 'pacific' *The Great Bear*

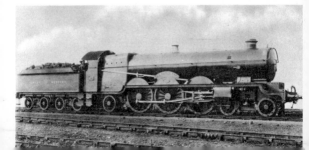

1909   SE&CR P Class 0–6–0Ts

What may be described as a more modern
version of the much better known Stroudley
'Terriers' described on page 38. Only eight of
these engines were built, but although possessing
no outstanding spectacular features, they warrant a
place in present-day history as four of them have
survived for preservation. They were lightweight
engines designed by Mr H. S. Wainwright for
working pull and push trains on branch line
workings. All were built at Ashford in 1909 and
1910, numbered 27, 178, 323, 325, 555, 558, 753 &
754. The last two later became 556 and 557.

Three of the four survivors are to be found in
working order on the Bluebell Railway. No. 27
is fully restored to SE&CR livery. No. 323 is now
known as *Bluebell*. No. 178 had been sold to
Bowater's Paper Mills, Sittingbourne, where it was
known as *Pioneer II*. The fourth engine, formerly
SE&CR 753/556, which later became SR 1556 and
finally BR 31556 had been sold to Hodson Mills,
Robertsbridge, where it had been named *Pride of
Sussex*. It has now been obtained by the Kent &
East Sussex Railway preservation society, in whose
stud it is No. 11.

Dimensions:
Driving wheels 3′ 9″   Cylinders 12″ × 18″   Pressure
160 lb   Weight 28½ tons

1911   Robinson 2–8–0s

Mr J. G. Robinson, who was Chief Mechanical
Engineer of the Great Central from 1900 to the end
of its independent existence in 1922, and who had
previously occupied a similar position on the Waterford Limerick & Western Railway in Ireland,

SE&CR Small
Wainwright
0–6–0T

designed some very fine locomotives for the enterprising GCR. This line had evolved from the Manchester, Sheffield and Lincolnshire by virtue of its London Extension.

In particular, his standard heavy freight engine of 1911 was destined to achieve much historic interest, as the design was adopted by the Government during the First World War for use in the various theatres of action abroad. Several hundred were built by outside firms for this purpose alone, apart from the 130 engines constructed by the GCR for its own use between 1911 and 1920. After the war the Government engines were disposed of, some to railways abroad, and at home the LNWR had 50, the Great Western 105, while the LNER eventually absorbed another 273 into its own stock along with the original Great Central engines. The class was again one of those commandeered for overseas service at the beginning of the Second World War; 92 of the LNER engines were sent abroad, some of them being the same ones which had done duty in 1917–18, being thus 'called-up' for the second time. In 1946 the LNER renumbered the class from 3500 onwards, provision being made for the return of some of the war service engines, but in fact none of them ever came back. Consequently the remainder of the class eventually became Nos. 3570 to 3920 with some gaps, altered in due course under nationalization by the addition of 60000. Withdrawal on a general scale of the LNER engines did not begin until 1959, but it may be mentioned that the last of those acquired by the Great Western, which had been Nos. 3000–3099 and 6000–6004 in that Company's lists, was scrapped in 1958 and

Robinson's well-tried 2–8–0 design for the GCR, many of which served overseas in both world wars

50 engines of the LNWR, which became Nos. 9616–9665 (some of which were later renumbered into the 9400s), had all gone as early as 1933.

A good deal of rebuilding took place in LNER days, resulting eventually in some seven different sub-varieties from the original design. From 1944 Mr Thompson rebuilt a number of them with raised framing, Walschaert's valve gear, and so on, giving them a much more modern appearance. However, some of them remained in approximately original condition to the end, and one of these has been preserved by BR, not at present on public view, but destined for Leicester museum.

Some of those sold out of service after the First World War went as far afield as Australia, where they were engaged on mineral work until quite recently. Efforts are being made by a group of preservationists to bring one of them back to this country, an ambitious and expensive project. If successful, it will probably go to Quainton Road.

Dimensions:
Driving wheels 4′ 8″ Cylinders (2) 21″ × 26″
Pressure 180 lb

Another outstanding design by Mr Robinson in the same year was his 4-6-2T for express suburban working, of which 30 were built, mainly for use in the London area from Marylebone, on the Aylesbury and High Wycombe lines. Another twelve came out under Sir Nigel Gresley's régime after the grouping in 1925 for the North Eastern. Regarded by many as one of the finest express tank engines ever built, it is a great pity that one was not retained after the last was withdrawn in 1960. Their final BR numbers were 69800–69842.

The Great Central has been slightly unfortunate in the field of preservation, and with only one other class besides the 2-8-0 represented, it has a very poor share. This is the 'Director' class 4-4-0 described on page 121.

1911 GWR Lightweight Passenger Engines

The modern outside cylinder 2-6-0 mixed traffic engine originated on the Great Western by Mr Churchward in this year. The idea was to have a general purpose engine with a wide range of possible uses, even express passenger in an emergency, but at the same time it was to be sufficiently light in weight to give it the maximum route availability over secondary lines. Eventually no fewer than 342 were built up to the year 1932. No. 5322 has been preserved and is now at the premises of the GWR Society at Didcot, and at least one is still in existence in Barry scrapyard.

General dimensions:
Driving wheels 5′ 8″ Cylinders 18½″ × 30″ Working pressure 200 lb

GWR 2–6–0, an important mixed traffic design

In 1936 it was found that further engines of this category were necessary, but Mr Collett, then loco superintendent decided that a 4–6–0 version would be more desirable. Two designs were prepared, differing slightly in dimensions, of which the overall weight was the most important according to the limitation of the lines over which they would be able to work. 100 engines of each variety were planned.

The larger of the two was the 'Grange' class, with a weight (engine only) of 74 tons. Only 80 of them were built, before the Second World War halted construction, Nos. 6800–6879, and none of these has survived. The smaller variety, the 'Manors', with a weight of 68 tons 18 cwt, intended

GWR 'Manor' class for secondary main line routes

for such routes as the Midland and South Western Junction and Cambrian main lines, was again interrupted by the war after the building of 20 engines only, Nos. 7800–7819, but in this case another ten, Nos. 7820–7829 did in fact appear as late as 1950. It had been planned that the whole series should run from 7800–7899.

This lot has been a little more fortunate. No. 7808 *Cookham Manor* in working order can be seen at Didcot, headquarters of the GWR Society, 7827 *Lydham Manor* on the Dart Valley, and 7819 *Hinton Manor* on the Severn Valley with one or two other possibles from Barry scrapyard.

Apart from the weights already quoted, the **general dimensions** are:
Driving wheels (both classes) 5′ 8″ Cylinders 18½″ × 30″ (Granges) 18″ × 30″ (Manors) with other varieties resulting in tractive efforts of, respectively 28875 lb and 27340 lb

1913 Great Central 'Directors' Great Central Railway

Robinson's later 4–4–0 express engines, the first ten of which came out in 1913. These were Nos. 429–438. They were named after Directors of the company, hence the title by which the whole class has always been known, although the later engines bore names of other derivation, and the original 429 and 437 subsequently became *Prince Henry* and *Prince George*.

A slightly enlarged version appeared in 1919 and eleven were built between that year and 1922. These were Nos 501–511. After the grouping another batch of 24 was turned out for use over the NBR lines in Scotland, for which purpose the boiler mountings were reduced in height to suit the more restricted loading gauge. These were LNER Nos. 6378 to 6401, and in 1925 all received names of Scottish origin. The GCR-built engines had 5000 added to their numbers. In 1946 the whole class was renumbered 2650–2694, which under BR auspices in due course was increased by 60000.

All were superheated from the start, and the chief visible later alterations consisted in the cutting away of the coupling rod splashers giving complete clearance to the rods, and there were one or two variations in the style of chimney.

One of the later variety, No. 506 *Butler Henderson* has been preserved by BR, and was in Clapham museum until this was closed in 1973. It is not certain at the moment where it will eventually reappear on public view, but possibly it will be transferred to the new Leicester museum.

Dimensions:
Driving wheels 6′ 9″   Cylinders 20″ × 26″   Pressure 180 lb

1913   GNR (Ireland) 4–4–0s

Five engines were built in 1913 and another three in 1915 for express services between Dublin and Belfast and until 1932 they were the largest to be found on

(*above*)
Robinson GCR
'Director' class

(*right*) Great
Northern of
Ireland.
Preserved
4–4–0 on a
steam rail tour
in September
1973

(*below*)
Somerset &
Dorset Derby
design of
2–8–0

the Great Northern of Ireland.   They were designed by G. T. Glover and built, as were most engines for that railway, by Beyer, Peacock & Co.   One of them, No. 171 *Slieve Gullion*, has been acquired by the Railway Preservation Society of Ireland and is frequently used on enthusiasts' specials, both in Northern Ireland and in the Republic.

Dimensions:
Driving wheels 6′ 7″   Cylinders 19″ × 26″   Pressure 200 lb

1914   Somerset & Dorset 2–8–0s

This railway was jointly owned by the Midland and the London & South Western Railways, and the former was responsible for the provision of motive power.   It was not surprising therefore that the locomotives were based largely on Derby practice, and the 2–8–0s introduced in 1914 by Sir Henry Fowler were pure Midland, although, strangely enough, that railway never built anything larger than a 0–6–0 for its own heavy freight traffic.   Six engines, Nos. 80–85, came from Derby in 1914, and in 1925 a further five, Nos. 86–90, were built by Stephenson & Co.

The S&DJR locomotive stock was absorbed into the LMS in 1930, and the 2–8–0s at first took the numbers 9670–9680, but they were soon afterwards altered to 13800–13810. On passing into BR hands they became 53800–53810.

The engines were built for working freight traffic over the steeply graded main line of the S&DJR between Bath and Bournemouth, on which route they spent their entire working life.   For a few months during 1918 No. 85 was lent to the parent Midland Railway which used it on coal trains between Wellingborough and Brent, with a view to constructing some for its own use, but nothing came of the idea. These engines remained at work until the early 1960s, when fortunately two of them found their way into Barry scrapyard and thus escaped the breaker's torch. One of these, No. 53808, old S&DJR No. 88, was rescued by the Somerset & Dorset Railway Circle in 1970 for preservation as the last example of one of the smaller railways of the country, and it is now housed in the old shed at Radstock, although not normally on public view.

Dimensions:
Driving wheels 4′ 8½″ Cylinders 21″ × 28″ Pressure 190 lb

1917 Maunsell 2–6–0s SE&CR and GSR (Ireland)

R. E. L. Maunsell had come to the SE&CR from the GS&WR of Ireland, where he had built his earliest locomotives. His first designs for the SE&CR were two engines of considerable importance, the first being a 2–6–0 mixed traffic engine and the second a 2–6–4T for passenger work (see page 128).

The outstanding feature of these designs, which did not attract much attention at the time, was the use of long valve travel. Churchward alone, on the GWR many years before, had realized the value of this, but no other engineer appreciated its significance until Maunsell came along. It was not until the locomotive exchanges of 1924–5 between the GWR, LNER, and LMS that its superiority became generally recognized, and since then it became normal practice in locomotive design.

The new SE&CR engine, No. 810, embodied

SE&CR Maunsell's first mixed traffic 2–6–0

much of Great Western practice, including the coned boiler, but there was a good deal of Midland there also, as shown in the design of the cab, tender and other details.

After extensive trials 15 more were built, Nos. 811–825. No. 822 was fitted with three cylinders. Largely to avoid unemployment at Woolwich Arsenal, the Government ordered 100 of the design to be built there after the termination of the First World War. Fifty of them were eventually acquired by the Southern Railway as A826–A875 (later 1826–1875). One of these, No. A866, was on view at Wembley Exhibition during 1924/5. Of the remainder it may be mentioned that six sets of parts were sold to the Metropolitan Railway and emerged as 2–6–4Ts, while another 20 went to the Great Southern of Ireland, who thus acquired a number of new engines of Maunsell's design after he had left that railway.

Five more of the 3 cylinder variety similar to No. 822 were constructed at Ashford, Nos. 876–880 and another 15 of the two cylinder engines between 1932 and 1934, numbered 1400–1414. In 1930 No. A816 was taken into Eastleigh works and underwent extensive experiments as a condensing engine, but it never ran in traffic, and was eventually reconverted to standard. These engines did a great deal of useful work on all sections of the Southern lines, particularly in the west of England. All lasted until the 1960s, and at the time of writing one, No. 31874, remains in Barry scrapyard, and efforts are being made to secure its preservation.

Dimensions:
Driving wheels 5′ 6″   Cylinders 19″ × 28″   Pressure 200 lb   (Cylinders 16″ × 28″ in the three cylinder version)

There was also a 6′ 0″ version, originating with the rebuilding of the 'River Tanks' as mentioned on page 128, but also some more, newly constructed, and one of these, No. 1618, is preserved privately and to be found at Tenterden, Headquarters of the Kent & East Sussex Railway. Again, there was a three cylinder variety of this class. Of the 20 almost identical 5′ 6″ engines on the Great Southern of Ireland, these were supplemented by another six built new at Inchicore in 1930 with 6′ 0″ wheels; many of both varieties lasted almost to the end of steam working in the country in the early 1960s.

SE&CR 2–6–4T version of 2–6–0 for express passenger duties

LMSR Fowler 2–6–4T

1917 2–6–4Ts

It was not until comparatively recent years that the 2–6–4T wheel arrangement began to be adopted for general suburban and semi main line express work. The type had originally appeared on the Great Central in 1916 with some inside cylinder engines, but these were designed for freight duties.

In 1917 Mr R. E. L. Maunsell had brought out a solitary example No. 790, concurrently with a 2–6–0 tender engine No. 810 (see page 125) and this remained the only example until after the grouping. Another 20, however, were built in 1925/6 (one with three cylinders in lieu of two), all named after rivers and intended for express passenger work on the South Eastern section, but after an unfortunate derailment at Sevenoaks in 1927 resulting in a severe accident, they were taken out of service and later rebuilt as 2–6–0 tender engines. The SR never again allowed this wheel arrangement on passenger work, although they did build some further examples with three cylinders confined strictly to freight duties. Meanwhile Sir Henry Fowler on the LMS had introduced the

Ultimate development of LMS 2–6–4T introduced by
BR in 1950

type which was to prove extremely successful on that
line.   125 were built of his original design, Nos.
2300–2424 and Sir William Stanier, who succeeded
Fowler in 1932, continued with his own modifications, the principal of which was the substitution of
a taper boiler for a parallel one; the design was also
continued by his successors, C. E. Fairburn and
H. G. Ivatt.

Ultimately the whole class consisted of 545
engines, numbered between 42050 and 42699
(exclusive of 42495–42499, which remained blank)
the last of which did not appear until after nationalization.   37 of them, Nos. 42500 to 42536, were built
with three cylinders and worked almost exclusively
on the LT&SR section.   The first of these, restored
as LMS 2500, is preserved and is to be found at
Bressingham Hall.   Unfortunately none of the
original Fowlers was retained, but two other late
ones which came out from Brighton in 1950/1 as
42073 and 42085, and which worked for a time on
the Southern Region, have been acquired by the
Lakeside Preservation Society.   The first mentioned
is rather curiously sporting the old Caledonian

Railway blue livery, and the other is in former LNWR lined-out black.

Thereafter the design was adopted with very few main differences as one of the twelve standard types for new construction by BR, and 155 further ones; Nos. 80000–80154, appeared between 1952 and 1957. A few of these have been secured by preservation societies, among which are 80002 in full working condition on the Keighley & Worth Valley Railway, 80064 on the Dart Valley, 80079 on the Severn Valley, 80105 is at the Falkirk premises of the Scottish Railway Preservation Society, and others are under negotiation from Barry scrapyard.

Dimensions remained much the same. All had 5′ 9″ driving wheels, the cylinders were 19″ × 26″ in the original Fowler engines, but became 18″ × 28″ in the BR standard, and the pressure increased from 200 lb to 225 lb.

A modified version of the original parallel boiler type with 6′ 0″ driving wheels was introduced in 1946 by the LMS for use on its Northern Counties section in Ireland, adapted of course to the 5′ 3″ gauge. 18 of these were built—NCC Nos. 1–10 and 50–57; No. 4 has been obtained by the Northern Ireland Preservation Society at Whitehead, Belfast, and is now used on occasions for enthusiasts' rail tours.

Another railway to adopt the 2–6–4T was the LNER, at the end of its existence, designed by Thompson and built between 1945 and 1950. These eventually became BR 67701–67800, but all had disappeared by 1962.

Reference should also be made to six engines which the Metropolitan Railway acquired from Woolwich (as mentioned on page 126) in an uncompleted form, or ('do-it-yourself' spare parts kits, in modern language) and converted by Armstrong Whitworth & Co. in 1924 to 2–6–4Ts, mainly for

Modified version of Fowler 2–6–4T for express work in Northern Ireland

freight working between Verney Junction and Neasden. They became Met 111–116 and were duly transferred to London Transport and later to the LNER.

1918   SR 'King Arthur' Class

What was later to develop into the well-known 'King Arthur' class originated with Mr R. W. Urie's express passenger 4–6–0, which he had introduced to the London & South Western in 1918. These in turn had sprung from his original 6′ 0″ mixed traffic design of 1914, revolutionary at the time by virtue of their high running plates, precursors of the pattern which was eventually to become more or less standard practice in the later and closing years of steam.

All of Mr Urie's 4–6–0s were a vast improvement on those of his predecessor, Dugald Drummond, whose somewhat clumsy and sluggish engines of this wheel arrangement were not among his most successful designs.

For the first time the L&SWR had a modern and

powerful express engine, and 20 of them, Nos. 736–755, were built between 1918 and 1923. After the grouping Mr Maunsell, now Chief Mechanical Engineer of the newly-formed Southern Railway, adopted the design with some modifications for his new 'King Arthur' class. The original Urie engines were incorporated in this and also given names associated with the Knights of the Round Table, as applied to the new engines, of which 54 were built, Nos. 448–457 and 763–806. They did yeoman service over all the divisions of the SR for many years, some of them until the early 1960s. No. 30777 *Sir Lamiel*, has been preserved and can be seen at the Ashford Steam Centre.

Dimensions:
Driving wheels 6′ 7″   Cylinders $20\frac{1}{2}″ \times 28″$ Pressure 200 lb

An express freight version with 5′ 7″ driving wheels of Mr Urie's design appeared from Eastleigh in 1920, 20 engines, Nos. 496–515 being built. One of them, No. 506, has been rescued from Barry scrapyard for preservation, the only Urie engine to survive.

Urie's design of express 4–6–0 subsequently incorporated in Maunsell's 'King Arthur' class

1919 Midland Railway Fowler 0–10–0 Banking Engine

The closing weeks of 1919 saw the appearance from Derby works of what was by far the largest locomotive ever to be built for the Midland Railway, which had remained a 'small engine' line during the period when most other railways had gone in for much larger and more powerful machines.

No. 2290 was a four cylinder 0–10–0 engine built especially for banking up the Lickey Incline with the two miles of continuous 1 in 37 ascent, and which had hitherto seen nothing larger than 0–6–0Ts on that duty. It was, moreover, the only ten-coupled engine in the country at the time, its only other predecessor in this respect having been the GER 'Decapod' (page 102), and it was not until 1943 that any further engines with ten wheels coupled appeared in Great Britain.

The new Midland locomotive had Walschaert's outside valve gear, and the two piston valves for the four cylinders had outside admission, the parts of the inside cylinders being crossed. The cylinders were steeply inclined.

To facilitate drawing up to the rear of a train in darkness, preparatory to banking, it was fitted with a powerful electric headlight. It spent almost the whole of its life on the duty for which it was built, although it made one or two early trials on mineral trains between Toton and Cricklewood. It remained the only representative of its class, and in order to ensure as short an absence as possible on its visits to workshops, it had two boilers which could be interchanged on these occasions. After 36 years of heavy pounding up the bank it was withdrawn from service in 1956. Its cylinders have been preserved. In 1947 it was renumbered 22290, and under the BR régime it became 58100. It went locally by the name of *Big Bertha*. Fortunately the impressive sound of its throaty exhaust has been preserved on a gramophone record by an enterprising firm specializing in railway recordings.

Regrettably the engine did not survive for the preservation it warranted, although efforts were made to save it.

Dimensions:
Driving wheels 4′ 7½″ Cylinders (4) 16¾ × 28″
Pressure 180 lb   Tractive effort 43315 lb

Big Bertha, the solitary MR 0–10–0 built for banking on the Lickey Incline

1922 Gresley 'Pacifics'

Apart from the solitary GWR *Great Bear* of 1908, no pacifics had been used in this country. At the end of 1922, at the close of the Great Northern Railway as a separate concern and before its absorption into the newly-formed LNER, two pacifics made their appearance and caused something of a sensation. They were a revolution in size and power for express working on the East Coast route main line,

Gresley's original 'pacific' for the GNR

hitherto entirely in the hands of the Ivatt and NER atlantics. The engines were destined to be the forerunners of two of the most famous classes ever to run in this country. They were followed in 1923 by ten further examples, at first numbered LNER 1472N–1481N and latterly 4472 to 4481. The 4472, later named *Flying Scotsman*, has become the best known of all, and after its recent sojourn in the USA, has now returned to this country to make periodic appearances on enthusiasts' specials. In 1925 No. 4474 underwent trials on the Great Western main line, matched against GWR 4–6–0, No. 4079 *Pendennis Castle* (also preserved, see page 107) as a result of which the class subsequently acquired 220 lb pressure boilers in lieu of their original 180 lb. They were followed up to 1935 by Nos. 2543–2582, 2743–2752, 2795–2797 and 2500–2508, mostly named after famous race horses. The class eventually became BR 60035–60112, together with 60113 which was in fact the original 1470; this had been rebuilt by Mr Thompson in 1945 and became the prototype of a new class of his own, numbered 60113 to 60162. With the exception of *Flying Scotsman* itself, the whole class was withdrawn between 1959 and 1964 as a consequence of rapid dieselization, and very regrettably no others have survived. Originally classified A1, they were latterly known as class A3.

Dimensions:
Driving wheels 6′ 8″   Cylinders (3) 19″ × 26″
Pressure 220 lb

1925 Garratt Engines

The largest and most powerful engine ever to run in the British Isles. What is in effect two engines in one, employing a single large boiler, was a patent of Beyer, Peacock & Co. of Manchester. This type of loco achieved very great success abroad, particularly in South Africa, where it can still be seen in considerable numbers. Its application in the British Isles has been extremely small. Apart from this solitary example, which was a 2–8–8–2 built for banking on the Worsboro' Incline near Barnsley, there were also 33 2–6–6–2s on the LMS, which came out in 1927–30 and were employed on heavy coal trains up to the 1950s. Its only other employ-

Britain's first main line Garratt engine built in 1925 for the LNER. Seen on the LMS Lickey Incline in 1949

(*upper*) LMS Garratt engine introduced in 1927 for main line freight traffic

(*lower*) Small Garratt engine for industrial service, *William Francis* at Baddesley Colliery

ment has been of a small 0–4–4–0 version of which a few were to be found on various industrial lines. One of these, built in 1937 and used at Baddesley Colliery, Warwick, has been preserved and can be seen at Bressingham Hall, Norfolk.

None of the main line engines has survived, but it may be mentioned that the very first Garratt of all, built by Beyer, Peacock & Co in 1909 for the Tasmanian Government Railways, was re-imported by the makers on its withdrawal in 1947 and exhibited at their works in Manchester. When the firm closed down in 1965 the locomotive was acquired by the Festiniog Railway, who hope eventually to restore it to working order on their own line.

Dimensions of LNER 2–8–8–2:
Driving wheels 4′ 8″ Cylinders (6) $18\frac{1}{2}″ \times 26″$
Pressure 180 lb Tractive effort 72940 lb Weight 178 tons

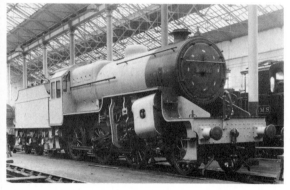

LMSR Hughes design for 2–6–0 for mixed traffic working on the LMS

1926 LMSR 2–6–0s

Designed by G. Hughes, the first loco superintendent of the LMS, who came from the Lancashire & Yorkshire Railway, and built at Horwich in 1926. The very high running plate was somewhat unusual at the time (although anticipated by Urie on the LSWR as early as 1914) but was destined to become common practice in future locomotive design.

245 of this useful mixed traffic class were built up to 1931, Nos. 13000–13244, later numbers 2700–2944 and BR 42700–42944. The original engine, now painted as LMS 2700, has been preserved by BR and is at present to be seen on the Keighley & Worth Valley Railway at Oxenhope.

Dimensions:
Driving wheels 5′ 6″   Cylinders 21″ × 26″   Pressure 180 lb

1926   SR 'Lord Nelson' Class

Maunsell's largest express passenger class, designed mainly for working Continental boat trains between Victoria and Dover.   The first engine, *Lord Nelson*, was built at Eastleigh in 1926, followed by another 15, all named after sea lords, in 1928/9.   The class was numbered 850–865.   They were unusual for a four cylinder type in that the driving axle cranks were set at 135° instead of the usual 90°, which resulted in the engine giving eight beats per revolution of the driving wheels in place of the usual four, with a consequent soft and smooth beat of the exhaust.   Not only were they very capable machines on the duties for which they were designed, but until later disfigured by smoke deflectors and more particularly wide chimneys necessitated by the use of multiple blast pipes, they were considered by some to rank among the most handsome 4–6–0s to run in this country.

The original engine has been retained by BR for preservation, but is not yet on public view.

Dimensions:
Driving wheels 6′ 7″   Cylinders (4) 16½″ × 26″
Pressure 220 lb

Maunsell's 'Lord Nelson' class 4–6–0 built mainly
for working continental boat trains

(*above*) LMS experimental high pressure *Fury*
(*below*) The *Royal Scot* on tour in Canada in 1933

By 1926 the London Midland & Scottish Railway was finding itself in increasing need of a large express engine for the West Coast route; the LNWR 'Claughtons' had never proved themselves really satisfactory for the top link duties, and the importation of some Hughes 4–6–0s from the L&YR section did not solve the problem. Sir Henry Fowler had already prepared plans for both a 3 cylinder compound 4–6–0 and a 4 cylinder compound pacific. Unfortunately these highly promising designs were vetoed by the Operating Department, and as new engines were needed in a hurry, recourse had to be made to a 3 cylinder simple 4–6–0. Accordingly the well-known 'Royal Scot' class appeared, the first 50, Nos. 6100–6149, all coming out in 1927, followed by Nos. 6150–6169 in 1930. A further experimental engine, No. 6399 *Fury*, was also built in 1930. This had a compound super pressure boiler of German design known as the Schmidt-Henshel type; it was a complicated affair with varying pressures, the maximum being no less than 900 lb per square inch. Unfortunately a boiler tube burst on trial, and an inspector on the footplate received fatal injuries. The engine was rebuilt with a taper boiler in 1935, becoming No. 6170 *British Legion*. Eventually all of the 'Royal Scots', which had originally been constructed with parallel boilers, were rebuilt in a similar manner. The complete class became BR 46100–46170.

In 1933, No. 6152 exchanged name and number with No. 6100, as the *Royal Scot* was sent to the USA for exhibition at Chicago. The numbers were not changed back on its return, and 46100 was therefore the same engine, although rebuilt with taper boiler, as went to America.

The *Royal Scot*, restored to maroon livery and with

its old number 6100, is preserved at Bressingham Hall, Diss, while another, No. 6115 *Scots Guardsman* is at Dinting, the premises of the Bahamas Loco Society.

Nos. 6125–6149 originally bore names commemorating early LNWR locomotives such as *Sanspareil*, *Samson*, *Novelty* and *Lion*, with brass plates bearing an etching of the locomotive represented, but in 1935–6 these were replaced by regimental names.

Dimensions:
Driving wheels 6′ 9″ Cylinders (3) 18″ × 26″
Pressure 250 lb

About the time of the unfortunate high pressure engine *Fury* already mentioned, Sir Nigel Gresley of the LNER had also been experimenting with similar ideas, although quite different in concept. His 'hush hush' engine, built under conditions of great secrecy in 1929, turned out to be a semi-streamlined 4–6–4, the only 'Baltic' tender engine ever to run in Great Britain, a four cylinder compound with a marine-type Yarrow boiler pressure to 450 lb. No. 10000 (it never bore a name) achieved a good measure of success and ran in this form for several years. It was however eventually rebuilt more or less in conformity with the A4 pacifics, although retaining its 4–6–4 wheel arrangement, and ran until 1959 as BR 60700.

Gresley's high pressure engine for the LNER

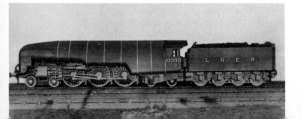

GWR 'Hall' class general-purpose design of mixed traffic 4–6–0 No. 6927 *Lilford Hall*

1928 GWR 'Hall' Class

In this year one of the 2 cylinder GWR 4–6–0s (see page 106) was rebuilt with smaller driving wheels (6' 0" in place of 6' 8½") to form a new design for general mixed traffic work. This was No. 2925 *Saint Martin*, which was renumbered 4900. The new class was eventually multiplied to 330 engines, Nos. 4900–4999, 5900–5999, 6900–6999 and 7900–7929, all named after English country seats known as *Halls*. Several have survived for preservation, or are in course of negotiation, among which are No. 4983 *Albert Hall* at Tyseley and 6960 *Raveningham Hall* at Steamtown, Carnforth. The only one yet restored to working order at the time of writing is No. 6998 *Burton Agnes Hall* at the GWR Society's premises at Didcot.

1929 GWR Saddle tanks

The introduction in this year of a standard design of 0–6–0 pannier tank by the Great Western Railway followed a traditional use of this type of engine for general-purpose duties extending back over very

Early GWR 'convertible' saddle tank as running in broad gauge form, otherwise typical of the very numerous class of engines on this railway dating back to the 1860s and used in great numbers for all kinds of work (Brunel's 7′ 0″ gauge was abandoned in 1892)

many years, which in fact started as early as 1860. From about the turn of the century right up to their gradual displacement by diesels this railway maintained a stock of about 1000 of this useful type. The earlier ones comprised a good many varieties; some of them were built with outside frames and there were various dimensional differences, but all but a very few conformed to the general pattern and had the distinctive round saddle tanks over the top of the boiler. In later years, from about 1909 onwards, many were rebuilt with the better known 'pannier' type, again carried by the boiler but consisting of two separate halves of rectangular shape. All of the new standard design built from 1929 onwards were of this type, and in all nearly 1000 were built up to the year 1956, gradually replacing the older ones. The new series again consisted of a number of variations for different types of work. These distinctive engines were an essential part of the GWR scene all over the system, and could be found on all kinds of duties ranging from humble shunting to anything short of a main line express, although they did a great deal of passenger work of an intermediate nature, particularly on branch and cross country lines. Many of them lasted well into the 1960s, and the last survivors of all were a few which had been sold to London Transport for departmental duties. These were still to be seen at work in the London area as late as 1971, three years after the cessation of steam working on British Railways.

At least a dozen have been acquired by various organizations for preservation in working order. They are mostly repainted in GWR livery, and can sometimes be seen in steam. Nos. 7752 and 7760 are at the Tyseley Steam Centre, Birmingham. No. 5786 is owned by the Worcester Loco Society, and can usually be seen at Bulmer's, Hereford, No. 7715 at Quainton Road, Nos. 5764 and 7714 on the Severn Valley Railway at Bridgnorth, and No. 5775 (carrying London Transport No. L89) on the Keighley & Worth Valley Railway. 3650 and 3738 are owned by the GWR Society at Didcot, 9642 is owned privately, and it is possible that others are still in existence. Four others, No. 1638 (with slightly smaller driving wheels) together with Nos. 6412, 6430 and 6435, which were built specifically for passenger work and fitted with pull and push apparatus, are to be found on the Dart Valley Railway.

Final standard development of the ubiquitous GWR saddle or pannier tank

1930 Schools Class   Southern Railway

Maunsell's last design of express passenger engine, and in many ways his finest achievement. The need had been felt for a locomotive with approximately the same haulage capacity as the 'King Arthurs' but with greater route availability, particularly as regards the SECR Hastings line with its restricted loading gauge. The resulting 'Schools' class may in some way be regarded as a 4–4–0 version of the 'Lord Nelsons' (see page 139), with two important differences: the use of three cylinders in place of four, and of a round-topped firebox in place of the Belpaire. The new engines quickly showed themselves as coming up to all expectations. In later years they did even more than had been anticipated when they were put to work on the heavy expresses between Waterloo and Bournemouth, after being displaced to some extent from the South Eastern section for which they were originally designed. They also did fine work over the Portsmouth road before electrification. With a tractive effort of only slightly less then the 4–6–0 'King Arthurs' (see page 132), they were the most powerful and one of the most successful 4–4–0 designs ever built in this country. They were incidentally the last new design of that wheel arrangement in Great Britain, although two others were yet to appear on the GNR of Ireland. In all, 40 were built between 1930 and 1935. Numbered 900–939, and were named after public schools. All lasted until the early 1960s, and three have survived for preservation.

No. 30925 *Cheltenham*, officially preserved by BR, is at the moment of writing to be found at the Dinting Railway Centre, Glossop, Derbyshire. No. 928 *Stowe*, restored to SR livery, was at first preserved by Lord Montague at his outdoor museum

SR Maunsell 'Schools' class 4–4–0 No. 922
Marlborough

at Beaulieu, Hants. It has now been moved to the headquarters of the Shepherd Railway Preservation Trust, Cranmore, Somerset, but it is not yet on public view. No. 926 *Repton* has gone far afield to the USA museum at Steamtown, Vermont.

Dimensions:
Driving wheels 6′ 7″ Cylinders (3) $16\frac{1}{2}$″ × 26″
Pressure 220 lb

1932   GWR 0–4–2Ts

The Great Western in its heyday had an unusually large number of short country branches, for the operation of which 0–4–2Ts had for many years, dating back to 1868, been a favourite choice. By the 1920s and 1930s these were becoming ancient and uneconomical for further repairs, so the railway constructed a large number of new ones of virtually the same design but with a few minor improvements. In all, 95 were built between 1932 and 1936, 75, Nos. 4800–4874, being fitted with pull and push apparatus, for auto working, and 20, Nos. 5800–5819, without. The auto engines were later renumbered 1400–1474, and four of these have survived for preservation: No. 1442, which stands on a pedestal at Tiverton, and three others in working order, No. 1466, owned by the Great Western Society at Didcot, together with 1420 and 1450 on the Dart Valley Railway.

1932　Great Northern of Ireland Compounds

Five engines appeared in 1932 for working the accelerated expresses between Dublin and Belfast which were introduced in that year. They were designed by Mr G. T. Glover, and built by Beyer, Peacock & Co. Numbered 83–87, and were named after birds. They were the last new compounds for any railway in the British Isles, and also among the last 4–4–0s (see page 173). No. 85 *Merlin* is preserved in Belfast Museum.

Dimensions:
Driving wheels 6′ 7″　Cylinders One inside, High pressure　17¾″ × 26″　Two low pressure outside 19″ × 26″
Pressure originally 250 lb later reduced to 215 lb

1933　LMS Pacifics

One of Mr (later Sir) W. A. Stanier's first tasks on being made Chief Mechanical Engineer of the LMS in 1932 was to set about the production of a really large main line engine for the West Coast route. His first two pacifics, No. 6200 *Princess Royal* and No. 6201 *Princess Elizabeth* introduced several new features to LMS practice, including the use of taper boiler, which he imported from Swindon, where he had previously been working. After thorough trials ten more, Nos. 6203–12, with slight modifications, came out in 1935.

No. 6202 was an experimental engine which differed radically from its sisters. The boiler, wheels, etc., were identical, but in place of normal cylinders and reciprocating motion it was propelled by turbines, a large one on the left-hand side of the engine, for forward motion, and a smaller one on the right-hand side for reverse running. It was not the first turbine-driven locomotive in this country. Other experiments in this direction had been made in the 1920s, but it was undoubtedly the only successful turbine design to appear. Many snags were encountered and the engine spent a good proportion of its life in the works undergoing modifications, but nevertheless when it was in service it was a very good engine and performed work equal to that of its orthodox sisters. It ran as a turbine engine until 1952, when it was rebuilt with a normal four cylinder propulsion. Previously nameless, it now became *Princess Anne*, but its life under its new metamorphosis was exceedingly short, as it was involved in the disastrous Harrow accident in that year, and was damaged beyond repair.

Two of these engines have survived, both restored to LMS maroon livery, No. 6201 at Ashchurch, Gloucestershire in working order, and No. 6203 *Princess Margaret Rose* on static exhibition at Butlin's Holiday Camp, Pwllheli, North Wales.

Dimensions:
Driving wheels 6′ 6″   Cylinders (4) $16\frac{1}{4}″ \times 28″$
Pressure 250 lb

Following the success of these engines, an improved design appeared in 1937 for working the newly inaugurated high speed service between London and Glasgow. These were fully streamlined, and although impressive were aesthetically extremely ugly. The shock of such unconventional appearance was somewhat diminished as Gresley's controversial streamlining on his own pacifics, two years earlier, had already paved the way. The new engines, Nos. 6220–6224, were painted blue, with horizontal white bands, to conform with the new coaching stock introduced on the new service.

LMSR *Princess Elizabeth*

LMSR Turbine pacific

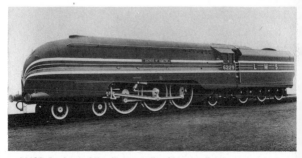

LMSR *Duchess of Hamilton* as built with streamlined casing

Nos. 6225–29, which followed, were however painted in standard LMS maroon. The next batch, Nos. 6230–6234 were non-streamlined and presented a handsome appearance. Further additions to the class were Nos. 6235–6248, all streamlined, and finally, between 1944 and 1948 there came Nos. 6249–6257 without streamlining. No. 6256 was named after its designer, *Sir William A. Stanier, FRS*. This, and No. 6257, had roller bearings. The outer casing was eventually removed from all the streamlined engines, as it was found to be of little value at speeds below 90 mph or so, and was a nuisance to the maintenance staff as it rendered parts of the engine inaccessible. To combat the trouble of drifting steam over the cab, all the class were fitted with smoke deflectors, but strangely this was never found to be necessary with the earlier 'Princess' class.

Prior to the introduction of the 'Coronation' flier in July 1937, No. 6220 was tried out with a special train and attained 114 mph just south of Crewe, thus beating the record of 113 mph at that time held by the LNER.

The 'Coronation' class proved themselves to be magnificent engines, not only in the realms of speed, but in their ability to handle the very heavy expresses

LMSR *Duchess of Sutherland*

over the West Coast route. On test in 1939, No. 6234, then newly fitted with a double chimney, worked a train of twenty coaches, 610 tons behind the tender, between Crewe and Carlisle, 102 miles in 118 minutes. This included of course the ascent of Shap. These engines remained as top link working on the West Coast main line until replaced by diesels.

In January 1939, No. 6229 *Duchess of Hamilton* was sent on exhibition to New York, and later made an extended tour over the USA railways. It was still there when war broke out, and was not returned to this country until 1943. During this time it had exchanged numbers and nameplates with No. 6220 *Coronation*, but these were altered back on the engine's return.

This engine is now to be seen on show at Butlin's Holiday Camp, Minehead. No. 6223 *Duchess of Sutherland* is at Bressingham Hall, Diss, and No. 46235 *City of Birmingham* still in BR green livery, at the Birmingham Museum of Science and Industry.

Dimensions:
Driving wheels 6′ 9″ Cylinders (4) 16¼″ × 28″
Pressure 250 lb

1934 LMSR Stanier 4–6–0s

Generally known under the soubriquet of Stanier 'Black Fives', these were undoubtedly the most efficient design of general-purpose mixed traffic engines this country has ever seen.

Introduced by Sir William Stanier in 1934 soon after his appointment as CME to the LMS, these engines quickly established themselves as a reliable design which could be used for almost every type of traffic. They were soon to be found all over the system from Wick in the far north to Bournemouth

LMSR Stanier 'Black Five'

in the south, over the lines of the Somerset & Dorset
Joint Railway.

Eventually no fewer than 842 of these were to
appear up to the year 1950, all of the same basic
design but with a few variations. 20 engines were
fitted with Caprotti valve gear in place of the usual
Walschaerts, and one with Stephenson's outside
link motion. The whole series eventually became
BR 44658–45499. All were still in service until 1959
and many of them worked until the last days of
steam working in 1968; twelve have survived for
preservation, some in working order. Details of
these follow at the end of this section.

The general design with certain modification was
adopted by BR as one of its twelve standard types
for future construction, and 172 of these had been
built by the time the decision to abandon steam had
been made. These engines were Nos. 73000–73171,
of which the last came out from Doncaster in 1957.
The same variations occurred as with the LMS
engines in that one batch had Caprotti valve gear.
The new BR locos were never so popular with
enginemen as their predecessors and only two have

survived: No. 73050 acquired by the Peterborough Railway Society and named *City of Peterborough*, and 73129, built at Derby 1956, one of the Caprotti lot, purchased by Derby Corporation for use on the Midland Railway Company Limited, a private preservation group inaugurated in 1969, which aims to operate a length of line at Ambergate.

Dimensions:

LMS engines
Driving wheels 6′ 0″   Cylinders 18½″ × 28″   Pressure 225 lb

BR engines
Driving wheels 6′ 2″   Cylinders 19½″ × 28″   Pressure 225 lb

LMS engines preserved, some in BR condition and others with former LMS numbers:

45000   Officially preserved by BR. Not at present on public view.
5025   Fully restored to former LMS livery, temporarily on the Keighley & Worth Valley Railway, but intended for the Strathspey Railway in Scotland.
45212   Keighley & Worth Valley Railway.
45110   Named *RAF Biggin Hill* on the Severn Valley Railway.
44871, 44932, 5231 and 5407   All at Steamtown, Carnforth.
5428   On the North Yorkshire Moors Railway, named *Eric Treacey*.
44767 (the engine fitted with Stephenson's valve gear)   At Steamtown, named in memory of the late *Cecil J. Allen*.
44806   On Lakeside Railway, Haverthwaite.
45305   At premises of Albert Draper, scrapbreaker, Hull.

1934 Stanier 'Jubilee' Class

Almost concurrently with the 'Black Fives' just described came a new design of express engine for all ordinary main line work on the LMS apart from the heaviest top link jobs, for which the 'Princess' class pacifics had already made their appearance. Incidentally the name 'Black Fives' was given to the mixed traffic locomotives as these assumed black livery from the start, whereas the new 'Jubilees' came into the category of main line expresses, to which the maroon, originating from the old Midland crimson lake, was still applicable.

The 'Jubilees' were 3 cylinder simple engines and were based on the existing 'Patriot' class, or 'Baby Scots', as they were sometimes known, a design of Sir Henry Fowler, of which 52 had been built since 1930. The most obvious difference lay in the taper boiler (which Stanier imported from GWR practice at Swindon) in place of the parallel type.

The new engines performed the duties for which they were designed extremely well, particularly on the lines of the former Midland Railway. Here they handled most of the principal express trains right through to more recent years, when they gradually became superseded by diesels. 191 were built, Nos. 5552–5742, with splendid names associated with the British Empire, as it was in those days, also including many noted admirals and commemorating some former warships; others revived names from engines of an earlier age.

They were in the main unaltered throughout their existence, apart from the provision of smokebox steam deflectors, but two of them, Nos. 5735–5736, received larger boilers in 1942, bringing them into line with the rebuilt 'Royal Scot' class.

Three examples have been saved for preservation

LMSR *Silver Jubilee* as first turned out in experimental black and chromium livery, not perpetuated

all in working order, and all restored to LMS condition in maroon livery.

5596 *Bahamas* To be seen at the Dinting Railway Centre, Glossop, Derbyshire.

5593 *Kolhapur*. To be seen at the Standard Gauge Steam Trust, Tyseley.

5690 *Leander* Acquired on behalf of the Midland Railway Company Limited, preservation society based at Derby.

Dimensions:
Driving wheels 6′ 9″ Cylinders (3) 17″ × 26″
Pressure 225 lb

1935 Gresley A4 Pacifics

When the question of providing a high speed service between London and Newcastle on the LNER in the early 1930s was being mooted, the possibility of using a diesel electric train was considered on the lines of the *Flying Hamburger* already in service in Germany. However, as it would have given neither the desired standard of comfort nor the requisite speed, the idea was dropped. It was decided to use conventional type of rolling stock with steam propulsion and a certain amount of streamlining to reduce wind pressure at the high speeds contemplated. Sir Nigel Gresley assured the directors that he could produce an engine and train which would amply cover the requirements. His *Silver Link*, which appeared in 1935, was an improved version of his already successful pacific*

Gresley A4 pacific *Dominion of New Zealand*

design, but greatly altered in appearance. The now familiar wedge-shaped streamline casing was certainly startling at the time.

The first four engines, Nos. 2509–2512, soon showed themselves fully capable of doing all that was required, and in 1937 further examples were built for working the even more ambitious high speed non-stop 'Coronation' between London and Edinburgh. Eventually the class consisted of 35 engines, Nos. 2509–2512, 4462–4469, 4482–4500, and 4900–4903. No. 4498 was named *Sir Nigel Gresley* after its designer.

The exploits of these remarkable engines is comparatively recent history and needs no elaboration here, but the 126 mph speed attained by No. 4468 *Mallard* in July 1938 remains a world record for

* Already described on page 135.

steam which can be substantiated. A claim of 127 mph by a Pennsylvania 'atlantic' in 1905 seems to have been based upon somewhat flimsy evidence and can hardly be accepted.

No. 4469 was destroyed at York in 1942 in an air-raid, but the remainder were renumbered 1–34 in 1946, although not in chronological order. They became BR 60001–60034 and all were still in service until replaced by diesels in the 1960s.

In the field of preservation they have fared very much better than their forerunners, the A3s, as six of them are still in existence, although two of these are not in this country.

The one holding the previously mentioned speed record, *Mallard*, is preserved officially by BR in its original condition and blue livery as No. 4468, complete with valances over the driving wheels restored; these had been removed from the whole class to give easier access to the motion. It was housed in Clapham Museum until closure in 1973, and will eventually reappear at the new York premises in 1975.

The others are preserved by various organizations in working order, not normally on public view except when brought out for enthusiasts' specials. These are *Bittern*, original 4464, but now running under its 1946 number 19, 4498 *Sir Nigel Gresley*, again restored to its original condition, and 60009 *Union of South Africa*.

To be found in Canada is 60010 *Dominion of Canada*, at Delson, Montreal, and 60008 *Dwight D Eisenhower*, is at the National Railway Museum, Wisconsin, USA.

Dimensions:
Driving wheels 6′ 8″ Cylinders (3) $18\frac{1}{2}″ \times 26″$
Pressure 250 lb

Following his production of new designs of express
and mixed traffic types of locomotives for the LMS
in 1933/4 (see pages 149 to 156), Sir William
Stanier now turned his attention to the need for a
standard heavy freight engine. His new '8000'
class amply justified itself from the start, and it was
adopted as a standard type for the needs of the War
Department at the outbreak of the Second World
War, when it was used both on the home railways
and overseas. Several hundred were built, and in
1944 the unique situation arose whereby engines of
purely LMS design were being built by all four
railways (as yet unnationalized) not only at the
LMS' own works at Crewe and Horwich, but by the
LNER at Doncaster and Darlington, GWR at
Swindon, and the SR at Eastleigh, Ashford and
Brighton, as well as by outside firms.

The engines which finally came into BR stock
bore numbers in the range between 48000 and 48775.
The class was one of the last to remain in any considerable numbers in the last days of BR steam, and
some of them were in active service right through to
the end. At the time of writing, two have definitely been secured for preservation, with the
possibility of at least one other from Barry scrapyard. One of them has a very interesting history.
No. 48773 was built by the NB Loco. Co. in 1940
(works No. 24607) as LMSR No. 8233, being
transferred to the War Department in 1941 as WD
307 and sent overseas, where it became Iran State
Railways No. 41–109. Returned to this country as
WD 70307 in 1952, it was repaired at Derby as
WD500 and sent to Longmoor, but in June 1957 it
was at Bicester. It was reabsorbed into BR stock
the same year, and was first allocated the number
90733 in error (following the 'Austerity' 2–8–0s with

which it was confused) but this was quickly altered to 48773, at the end of the LMS 2–8–0s. It was withdrawn in 1968 and acquired by the Stanier 8F Locomotive Society. Restored as LMS 8233, it works on the Severn Valley Railway.

Another one, No. 8431, built at Swindon in 1944, is on the Keighley & Worth Valley Railway.

Dimensions:
Driving wheels 4′ 8½″ Cylinders 18½″ × 28″ Pressure 225 lb

LMSR Stanier class 8 2–8–0

1936 Gresley's 'Green Arrow' Mixed Traffic Engines

Sir Nigel Gresley's general purpose heavy main line locomotives, of which 184 in all were built between 1936 and 1944, numbered 4771 to 4899, and 3641 to 3695, eventually to become BR 60800 to 60983.

The fact that their construction continued through the war years well indicates their value in helping to cope with the additional traffic over the heavily used East Coast main line under the difficult wartime conditions, so much so that they have occasionally been described as the engines which 'helped to win the war'. They were sometimes to be seen on mammoth passenger trains of over 20 coaches, and while not intended for top link express duties they were quite capable of performing them when required. Their chief sphere however lay in the operation of fast express freight trains, the first engine being named after the inauguration of a new service of this nature. They put in some magnificent work until supplanted in the 1960s by the inevitable diesels.

The original *Green Arrow* has been preserved, restored to LNER condition, and although not normally on general public view, has been renovated into working condition and can be seen on occasional enthusiasts' steam specials. The 2–6–2 tender engine has never been a type to be used much in this country. The only other examples were a lightweight version of the Green Arrows by Gresley, of which two were built in 1941, but never multiplied in consequence of the designer's death, and the experimental Paget on the Midland mentioned on page 113.

Dimensions:
Driving wheels 6′ 2″ Cylinders (3) $18\frac{1}{2}″ \times 26″$
Pressure 220 lb

LNER *Green Arrow*

Great Southern Railways of Ireland No. 800 *Maeve*

1939 Great Southern Railways (Ireland) 4–6–0s

The last new steam engines (apart from Bulleid's experimental turf burner, see page 176), were built for the GSR, or Coras Iompair Eireann, as it later became.

These three engines bore the names of former Queens of Ireland; 800 *Maeve*, 801 *Macha* and 802 *Tailte*. They had a remarkable resemblance to the rebuilt Royal Scots of the LMS. They worked on the principal expresses between Dublin and Cork until dieselization in the early 1960s. No. 800 is preserved in Belfast Museum.

Dimensions:
Driving wheels 6′ 7″ Cylinders (3) $18\frac{1}{2}″ \times 28″$
Pressure 225 lb

1941 Southern Railway Bulleid Pacifics

The first engine of the 4–6–2 type to run on the Southern system appeared under conditions of some secrecy owing to war conditions during 1941. It was a 3 cylinder engine incorporating many novel features, including a thermic syphon, only once before used in this country, and a patent valve gear of O.V. Bulleid's own design in which the primary drive is by means of chains enclosed in an oil bath. It was fully streamlined, or air smoothed, as it was referred to at the time. Under a new numbering scheme devised by Mr Bulleid the first engine, named *Channel Packet*, was No. 21C1, the 21C representing the continental system of describing the wheel arrangement which would ordinarily have here been called 4–6–2, by the number of axles, the driving wheels being represented by the letter C following the bogie and trailing pony truck.

Twenty of these engines came out up to 1945. Somehow construction was permitted even though they were essentially express passenger locomotives and hardly necessary under war conditions. In some ways Bulleid managed to convince the authorities that they were essential to the prosecution of the war. Ten more followed after nationalization in 1948, with conventional numbers, 35021–35030, and the original ones duly became 35001–35020. They were known as the 'Merchant Navy' class, all bearing names of famous shipping lines.

These engines did a great deal of heavy main line service on the SR, but the valve gear was not entirely satisfactory, and beginning with No. 35013 in 1956, this was replaced by the Walschaert type. At the same time the streamlined casing was removed, which considerably improved the look of the locomotives. Their original boxed-in appearance had caused them to be irreverently described as 'spam cans'. All engines in the class were eventually so rebuilt.

A slightly lighter edition of the 'Merchant Navy' class, with greater route availability but embodying all the same features, came out between 1945 and 1949, Nos. 21C101–21C170 and 34071–

34110, the former becoming 34001–734070 under nationalization. Nos. 34001–34048 and 34091–34108 bore names associated with the West Country; most of the others had wartime commemorative names, chiefly after air squadrons which took part in the Battle of Britain, which title is sometimes applied as a class name to these particular locomotives. Rebuilding of this class on the same lines as the 'Merchant Navy' commenced in 1957, but

Southern Railway *Sir Winston Churchill*

only 55 of these, exactly half the total number, were so treated. All of both 'Merchant Navy' and 'West Country' classes were in active service until well into the 1960s, many of them until the end of steam working on the Southern Region in 1967. It was an ironic circumstance that of all railways in the country, the Southern, and particularly the London & South Western section which had been the pioneers in the promotion of electrification, should have been the last main line in the country to have remained entirely dependent upon steam. Right up to July 1967 steam trains were used on the

London, Bournemouth and Weymouth lines until the abrupt and complete change over to electrification was made in one fell swoop. The exploits of the Bulleid pacifics in efficiently fighting a magnificent rearguard action in their closing days, in spite of sad neglect of maintenance, deserves an honoured place in the history of the British steam locomotive.

As might be expected, these engines have not been neglected in the preservation field.

Southern Railway 'Merchant Navy' pacific de-streamlined

Most important of all, No. 21C151, which bears the honoured name of *Winston Churchill*, was one of those which was never rebuilt and retained its streamlined condition. It is officially preserved by British Railways, although not at the time of writing on public view. No. 34023 *Blackmore Vale* is on the Bluebell Railway, and No. 34039 *Boscastle* is at the headquarters of the Main Line Steam Trust, Loughborough, both of these in working order. 34092 *City of Wells* is on the Keighley & Worth

Valley, and 34016 *Bodmin* at Quainton Road. Others under negotiation are 34081 *92 Squadron* and 34105 *Swanage*.

Of the 'Merchant Navy' class, No. 35028 *Clan Line* is at the Ashford Steam Centre, 35005 *Canadian Pacific* at Carnforth, and there are one or two others in Barry scrapyard which may be saved from the breakers.

Dimensions:
Driving wheels 6′ 2″ Cylinders (3) 18″ × 24″ Merchant Navy; 16¾″ × 24″ West Country Pressure 250 lb

1942 Bulleid 'Austerity' 0–6–0s

This had the somewhat dubious reputation of being just about the ugliest engine ever seen on a British railway. It was one of Bulleid's contributions to the war effort and he achieved admirably his aim of producing an all-purpose engine under wartime conditions attaining maximum power with minimum weight and the widest possible route availability.

Southern Railway Bulleid 'austerity' 0–6–0

All frills were dispensed with, and the absence of any kind of running plate was just one of the stark innovations which reduced the finished product to what amounted to almost the ultimate limits of austerity without any pretence of aesthetic conditions. Nevertheless they were most efficient machines despite their somewhat ferocious appearance.

40 of them were built at Brighton and Ashford works during 1942, numbered C1 to C40 under Mr Bulleid's again unorthodox numbering scheme, later to become BR 33001–40.

The original engine has been officially preserved by BR but is not at present on public view.

Dimensions:
Driving Wheels 5′ 1″   Cylinders 19″ × 26″   Pressure 230 lb

1943   War Dept 'Austerity' 0–6–0STs and 2–8–0s

A standard shunting engine designed by the Hunslet Engine Co. for the War Department for use both at home and overseas, and turned out by various makers in large numbers between 1943 and 1953. Many of them were sold out of service after the war to collieries and other industrial concerns, and 75 were purchased by the LNER. More recently some have been acquired by various preservation societies, for which their simple and robust construction makes them admirably suitable. A few have been retained by the military authorities, and are to be found at some ordnance depots, although now only used on special occasions, as they have been supplanted by diesels. Of these, Army 92 *Waggoner* and 98 *Royal Engineer* are at Long Marston, and 197 *Sapper* is at Bicester. On the preserved

WD design of saddle tank for wartime use. One of the engines subsequently obtained by the LNER

lines, one of those which went to the LNER as 8077 (later BR 68077), together with two or three others, are now on the Keighley & Worth Valley Railway. 150 *Warrington* is at Dinting, 90 *Castle Hedingham* on the Stour Valley, 94 on the Lakeside Railway, together with others on the Kent & East Sussex Railway and at Quainton Road. Some also still remain at work in industrial service at collieries and elsewhere.

Principal dimensions: Driving wheels 4′ 3″ Cylinders 18″ × 26″ Pressure 170 lb

Another class of engine built specially for the Ministry of Supply for wartime needs, designed by Mr W. A. Riddles, appeared in 1943. This was a 2–8–0 freight engine, and these were turned out in very large numbers by the North British Loco. Co. and the Vulcan Foundry. In all, something like 900 of the class were built in three years. They were usually known as the *Austerities* owing to their simple construction. Many were used on the main lines of this country during the war to overcome the

Riddles design of 2–8–0 for wartime needs

shortage of engines.   200 were taken over by the LNER in 1946 and others were disposed of abroad. Eventually no fewer than 733 came into possession of British Railways, numbered 90000–90732, and it is strange that none of these survived the holocaust of the 1960s; not even a single one got to Barry scrapyard.   However, one of them, which had eventually finished up on the Swedish State Railways was recently discovered hibernating in sub-zero temperatures in a shed in the far north and brought back to England by the Keighley & Worth Valley Railway.   It has had an interesting history.

It was built by the Vulcan Foundry in 1945 as WD 79257, went to Holland and became Dutch State 4464, and in 1952 sold to the Swedish State, their number 1931.   Now to be seen at Haworth, it is fortunate that the most numerous class to run on British Railways has a representative specimen preserved.

Principal dimensions:
Driving wheels 4′ 8½″   Cylinders 19″ × 28″   Pressure 225 lb

There was also a 2–10–0 version of the design built at the same time, of similar dimensions and tractive effort, but heavier in weight, of which 150 were built.   One has survived.   This became WD 73651, later 600 and named *Gordon*.   It was preserved at Longmoor, Hants, until that army training centre was closed, and was acquired by the Transport Trust, and can now be seen on the Severn Valley Railway.

H. G. Ivatt's post-war design of light 2–6–0

1946

Two years before nationalization, in 1948, Mr H. G. Ivatt of the LMS introduced two lightweight designs, a tender and a tank version, mainly for cross country and branch line working, almost the last new types to appear on that railway.   20 of the 2–6–0s were initially built, Nos. 6400–6419, and ten of them 2–6–2Ts, 1200–1209, but both types were added to after nationalization with the construction of Nos.

46420–46527 and 41210–41329. The design was perpetuated by BR with very slight modifications and incorporated into the 12 standard classes adopted for future construction, as the 78000 and 84000 classes.

Several of each type have survived for preservation, mostly in working order, such as 46443 and and 46521 on the Severn Valley Railway, 6441 (so numbered and in LMS maroon livery, although it never ran originally in this condition) at Carnforth, 46447 at Quainton Road, and 46464 a static exhibit intended for Dundee museum. Of the 2–6–2Ts,

H. G. Ivatt's post-war design of light 2-6–2T

41241, again painted in LMS maroon, is in regular use on the Keighley & Worth Valley Railway, 41298 at Quainton Road, with one or two others such as 41312 from Barry scrapyard in negotiation.

Principal dimensions: applicable to both classes Driving wheels 5′ 0″   Cylinders 16″ × 24″   Pressure 200 lb

Great Northern of Ireland 4–4–0 No. 204 *Antrim* built
in 1947 to a 1915 design

1948 Great Northern of Ireland 4–4–0s

As late as 1948 five new 4–4–0s from the works of
Beyer, Peacock & Co appeared on the GNR for
express working between Dublin and Belfast, and
were notable in being the last engines of this wheel
arrangement to be built for use in Great Britain and
Ireland, and possibly in the whole world. They
were similar in some respects to the compounds of
1932 (see page 149), but with three cylinder simple
propulsion. They were numbered 206–210 and
named after Irish rivers. Their lives were comparatively short as dieselization ousted them in the
early 1960s.

Dimensions:
Driving wheels 6′ 7″ Cylinders (3) 15¼″ × 26″
Pressure 220 lb

It is interesting also to mention that in the previous
year, 1947, five other new 4–4–0s for lighter cross
country work had also appeared from Beyer,

Peacock, who built so many of this company's engines. These were of an old design dating back to 1915, with practically no alteration apart from rather more modern tenders. With inside cylinders and all the hallmarks of a couple of generations earlier, the appearance of new engines of what amounted to genuine Edwardian appearance was somewhat remarkable at such a late period.

Dimensions:
Driving wheels 5′ 9″ Cylinders 18″ × 24″ Pressure 200 lb

1949 Bulleid 'Leader'

Although designed by O. V. Bulleid during the last days of the Southern Railway, this remarkable locomotive did not appear until after nationalization. Nothing so revolutionary in steam locomotive design had been seen since the Midland Paget engine of 1908 (page 113). It incorporated many novel features, among which may be mentioned the sleeve type valves, and the coupling of the six wheels comprising each bogie by means of a chain transmission instead of coupling rods.

The engine may be briefly described as a 0-6-6-0 single boiler articulated unit completely enclosed by an overall casing. There was a cab at either end with duplicated controls, and the fireman had to work amidships alongside the boiler, the longitudinal axis of which was offset to one side of the centre line of the engine. Herein lay one of the principal defects of the design, in that the poor fireman was expected to work under almost impossible conditions such as few would be prepared to tolerate in these days. In this connection it would have probably been far more satisfactory if the engine had been constructed as an oil burner.

(*upper*) Bulleid's experimental *Leader* design for the Southern
      Railway
(*lower*) Bulleid's last experiment in steam propulsion, a turf
      burning engine for Coras Iompair Eireann of Ireland

Each bogie had a 3 cylinder engine driving the
middle wheels of each 3 axle bogie.

It was planned initially to build five of these
engines, but only three, Nos. 36001–3 were actually
constructed, and only the first one ever steamed.
After a few desultory trials the authorities seemed to
lose interest and all three engines were quietly

broken up after a very brief existence. The initial faults were many, as would be expected with such an unorthodox machine, but all could have been rectified with perseverance. If the matter had been pursued, the engines might have proved a revolution in railway motive power and even might have done something to stem the tide of dieselization and electrification which has since taken place. It may now be regarded as a last, and as it turned out, unsuccessful effort to prolong the use of steam propulsion as a factor of major importance in railway haulage.

It was not, however, Mr Bulleid's final fling. Finding himself redundant as a result of nationalization, he went to Ireland as Chief Mechanical Engineer of Coras Iompair Eireann, and proceeded to experiment with a somewhat similar locomotive, but designed to burn turf (or peat, of which there are large natural deposits in that country, but virtually no coal). Something might have been made of this, but the Irish railways were already turning their thoughts strongly towards dieselization, even before British Railways got around to it, and Mr Bulleid's ideas were destined to prove abortive.

Dimensions:
Driving wheels 5′ 1″   Cylinders (6) 12¼″ × 15″
Pressure 280 lb   Tractive effort 26350 lb   Weight 100 tons (approx)

1951 British Railways 'Britannia' Class

In 1950 when there was still no thought of general dieselization, BR under the locomotive superintendency of R. H. Riddles, assisted by E. S. Cox, evolved a plan for large scale production of twelve standard designs of steam locomotives over the following decade. The first to appear was a large 'pacific' for main line working, of which the initial example, No. 70000, appeared in 1951, followed by others, eventually totalling 55, Nos. 70000–70054. The engines were subject to a certain amount of criticism on their first appearance, but over the years of their comparatively short lives they acquitted themselves

The first BR standard design, Britannia class pacific

admirably. In particular they did extremely well over the difficult main lines of the old Great Eastern Railway, but they were to be found on express duties on most other principal routes of the system.

No. 70000 *Britannia* itself was withdrawn from service in 1966, and has been restored to working order, at present to be found on the Severn Valley Railway. A second engine, No. 70013 *Oliver Cromwell*, the last locomotive to receive a general overhaul by BR, ran until the end of steam in August 1968, hauling many enthusiasts' specials, after which it was acquired by Mr Alan Bloom and has found a permanent resting-place at his extensive indoor and outdoor museum at Bressingham Hall, Diss.

Dimensions:
Driving wheels 6′ 2″ Cylinders (2) 20″ × 28″
Pressure 250 lb

1951 British Railways Mixed Traffic 4–6–0

One of the twelve standard designs planned by BR for future construction before the 1956 decision to abandon steam propulsion.   In conformity with the current practice, it was of simple construction and the working parts were readily accessible for ease of maintenance; it was designed with medium axle load, intended chiefly for cross country and secondary lines.   It was found mainly on the Southern, Western and Midland Regions, including such routes as those of the former Cambrian Railway.

Eighty of them were built, Nos 75000–75079, of

BR intermediate design for 4–6–0 for lighter passenger duties

which No. 75027 may now be found at work on the
Bluebell Railway, No. 75029 owned by the Shepherd
Railway Preservation Trust, and named *The
Green Knight* (not at present on public view) together
with No. 75078 on the Keighley & Worth Valley
Railway and 75069 on the Severn Valley Railway.

Dimensions:
Driving wheels 5′ 8″   Cylinders 18″ × 28″   Pressure
225 lb

1954   Class 9 2–10–0s

This was the last of the twelve BR standard designs
to appear, the first example of which came out in
1954.   A large 2–10–0 engine intended in the main
for heavy mineral traffic, these locomotives were on
occasions used with considerable success on passenger trains, although not as a regular thing.   A
speed of 90 mph was recorded on at least one
occasion, an extraordinary figure for a ten-coupled
engine with wheels of only 5′ 0″ diameter.   In all,
251 engines of this class were turned out, Nos.
92000–92250.   The final one actually built was
No. 92220, which appeared from Swindon in March
1960 and was appropriately named *Evening Star*.
This was the last new steam locomotive constructed
for British Railways.

Nos. 92020–92029 were built experimentally with
Franco-Crosti type double boilers, a peculiarity of
these engines being that the chimney was used only
when the locomotive was being lighted up from cold,
the normal exhaust coming from a separate outlet
midway along the left-hand side of the boiler.
No. 92250 was fitted with an experimental type of
chimney embodying a device known as the Giesl
ejector.   This had been used extensively in Austria,

Evening Star, the last new steam engine for British Railways

and was said to give remarkable results in economy of coal consumption. Unfortunately this invention appeared too late on the scene to result in any appreciable prolongation of life of the steam locomotive in this country. Probably the best of all the BR standard designs, these fine engines had a regrettably and entirely uneconomic life span, as a result of the undue haste with which the dieselization programme was pushed forward in the 1960s.

Evening Star itself, on withdrawal in 1965 after a regular life of only five years, was officially preserved by British Railways and can in fact still be seen working trains on the Keighley & Worth Valley Railway, where it is at present on loan.

Two more examples have been acquired for preservation in working order: No. 92203 by David Shepherd, which has been given the name *Black Prince*, and is not at present on public view, and No. 92212 which is likely to be obtained by the Severn Valley Railway.

Dimensions:
Driving wheels 5′ 0″ Cylinders (2) 20″ × 28″
Pressure 250 lb

Principal Museums with Static Locomotives on Display

British Railways
York, new premises due to be opened in 1975 embodying the collection in the existing museum opened by the LNER in the 1930s (not at present on view) and most of the engines displayed in Clapham Museum, London, until closure in 1973.

Great Western Museum, Swindon.

* * *

Science Museum, Kensington, London
Glasgow Transport Museum
Belfast Transport Museum
Municipal Museums at Edinburgh, Newcastle, Hull, Liverpool, Birmingham, Leicester
Lytham Motive Power Museum, Lytham St Annes, Lancs
Bangor (Caernarvonshire) Industrial Railway Museum
Brockham Narrow Gauge Museum, Dorking, Surrey

Privately Owned Steam Centres at which steam locomotives are to be found, over which engines may be seen at times sometimes in steam, usually at weekends during the summer season.

Standard Gauge Steam Trust, Tyseley, Birmingham
Steamtown, Carnforth, Lancs
South Eastern Steam Centre, Ashford, Kent
Bressingham Hall, Diss, Norfolk (*open Thursdays & Sundays, May–September*)
Great Western Society, Didcot, Taunton, and Bodmin

Quainton Road Society, Quainton Road, Bucks

Dinting Railway Centre, Glossop, Derbyshire

Scottish Railway Preservation Society, Falkirk

Strathspey Railway, Aviemore, Inverness (*not yet operational*)

Bulmer's Cider Railway, Hereford

North Norfolk Railway Company Limited, Sheringham, Norfolk

Stour Valley Railway, Chappell & Wakes Colne, Essex

Shepherd Railway Preservation Trust, Cranmore, Somerset (*not at present open to the public*)

Somerset & Dorset Railway Circle, Radstock, Somerset

Dean Forest Railway Preservation Society, Parkend, Glos

Dowty Railway Preservation Society, Ashchurch, Glos

Yorkshire Dales Railway Society, Skipton, Yorks

Severn Valley Railway, Bridgnorth, Salop

Fully Operational Lines, some several miles in length, over which steam trains are run to established timetables, generally during weekends in the summer season.

Keighley & Worth Valley Railway, Haworth, Yorks (*runs all the year round service on Saturdays*)

North Yorkshire Moors Railway, Grosmont, Yorks

Dart Valley Railway, Buckfastleigh, Devon

Torbay Steam Railway, Paignton—Kingswear (worked by Dart Valley Ry) *daily service.*

Main Line Steam Trust, Loughboro', Leics

Bluebell Railway, Sheffield Park, Sussex

Tenterden Railway Company (Kent and East Sussex, Robertsbridge)

Middleton Railway, Leeds

Midland Railway Company Limited, Derby and Ambergate (*not yet operational*)

Foxfield Light Railway, Cheadle, Staffs

Chasewater Light Railway, Brownhills, Staffs
Lakeside and Haverthwaite Railway, Lancs
Lochty Railway, Fife, Scotland
Isle of Wight Steam Centre, Haven Street, Isle of Wight

Narrow gauge lines—Summer Season
Talyllyn Railway (*daily service*)
Festiniog Railway (*daily service*)
Vale of Rheidol (British Railways) (*daily service*)
Welshpool and Llanfair
Isle of Man Railway (*Monday to Friday only*)
Llanberis Lake Railway (*daily service*)
Fairbourne Railway (*daily service*)
Snowdon Mountain (rack rail) (*daily service*)
Ravenglass and Eskdale (*daily service*)
Leighton Buzzard Light Railway
Whipsnade Zoo Railway (*daily service*)
Romney, Hythe and Dymchurch Railway (*daily service*)
Sittingbourne and Kemsley Light Railway
Lincolnshire Coast Light Railway, Humberstone
Bicton Woodland Railway, Budleigh Salterton, Devon
Cadeby Light Railway, Nuneaton
West Lancashire Light Railway, Hesketh Bank, Preston
Shanes Castle Railway, Antrim, Ireland

*A full timetable and guide of all of the above lines is published
by David and Charles, Newton Abbot, Devon.*

Other projects are as yet only in the planning stage,
and include the reopening of the Taunton to Minehead
(West Somerset Railway Company Limited), the
Wareham and Swanage branch, Cranmore to Shepton
Mallet section of the GWR Cheddar Valley line, the
Peterborough Railway Society (Peterborough to
Wansford), Dean Forest Railway Preservation Society
(Lydney to Parkend), the Bristol Suburban Railway
(Bristol—Yate, Bath) Shackerstone (Leics) to Market
Bosworth, on all of which, if the plans materialize, it is
intended to make use of steam locomotives.

Index

Barry Railway
    0–8–0s, 76
Birmingham & Gloucester
    Norris 2–2–0s, 19–21
British Railways
    'Britannia' pacifics, 176–8
    2–10–0s, 179–80
    Class 5 4–6–0s, 155, 156
    Mixed traffic 4–6–0s, 178–9
    2–6–4Ts, 130
    2–6–2Ts, 172
    2–6–0s, 172

Caledonian Railway
    4–2–2, 69–70
    Dunalastair 4–4–0s, 84–5
    'Cardean', 85
Cambrian Railways
    Vale of Rheidol, 105–6
    Welshpool & Llanfair, 111
Canterbury & Whitstable
    'Invicta', 16
Coras Iompair Eireann
    Bulleid Turf burner, 175, 176

Festiniog Railway Fairlie engines, 36–7
Furness Railway
    'Coppernob', 23

Glasgow & South Western Railway
    4 cylinder 4–4–0, 86, 87
Great Central Railway
    4–4–0 Directors, 121–2, 123
    4–6–2Ts, 119
    2–8–0s, 116–19

Great Eastern Railway
    'Claud Hamilton' 4–4–0s, 94–5
    4–6–0s, 96
    J67 0–6–0Ts, 104–5
    N7 0–6–2Ts, 104–5
    Decapod, 102–4
Great Northern Railway
    Stirling 8 footers, 37–8
    Atlantics, 90, 91
    Pacifics, 134–5
Great Northern of Ireland Railway
    4–4–0s, 122–4, 148, 149, 173–4
Great North of Scotland Railway
    4–4–0s, 74, 75
Great Southern & Western Railway
    Bury 2–2–2, 23
    J15 0–6–0s, 33–4
Great Southern Railways
    Maunsell 2–6–0s, 126, 127
    'Queen' class 4–6–0s, 163
Great Western Railway
    Broad gauge
    'North Star', 17–18
    'Lord of the Isles', 18
    'Tiny', 56
    Standard gauge
    0–6–0STs & 0–6–0PTs, 143–5
    0–4–2Ts, 147–8
    Dean 0–6–0s, 67–8
    4–4–0s, 87–8
    4–6–0s, earlier Dean and Churchward 'Saints' &
       'Stars', 106–7
    4–6–0s 'Castles', 107, 108, 115, 135
    4–6–0s 'Kings', 107–9
    4–6–0s 'Halls', 143
    4–6–0s 'Granges' and 'Manors', 120–1
    'The Great Bear', 114–15
    2–6–0s, 119–20
    2–8–0s. 108, 109
    2–6–2Ts, 109–10

Hetton Colliery loco, 11–12, 13

Highland Railway
    Jones 4–6–0s, 82–3
Hull & Barnsley Railway
    0–8–0s, 78

Industrial locomotives, 42–3, 44, 56, 57, 65, 66, 137
Isle of Man Railway, 41–2
Isle of Wight Railways, 78, 79–80

Killingworth Colliery and Wagonway, 15, 16

Lancashire & Yorkshire Railway
    Atlantics, 91–2
    2–4–2Ts, 74–5
    Barton Wright 0–6–0s and 0–6–0STs, 55–6
Liverpool & Manchester Railway
    'Rocket', 11, 12, 14
    'Lion', 18–19
London Brighton & South Coast Railway
    Stroudley 'Terriers', 38–40
    'Gladstones', 60–2
London Midland & Scottish Railway
    4–4–0 Compounds, 100–2
    Hughes 2–6–0s, 138–9
    Fowler 0–6–0Ts, 49–50
    Fowler 0–6–0s, 52–4
    Fowler 0–8–0s, 79
    Fowler and Stanier 2–6–4Ts, 128–30
    Stanier 2–8–0s, 160–1
    Royal Scots, 140, 141–2
    'Black Five' 4–6–0s, 153–5
    'Jubilee' 4–6–0s, 156–7
    Pacifics, 149–53
    Ivatt 2–6–0s and 2–6–2Ts, 171–2
    Garratts, 136, 137
    Northern Counties Committee, 2–6–4Ts, 130, 131
London & North Eastern Railway
    Garratt, 136
    Gresley Pacifics, 134–5, 136, 157–9
    No 10000, 142
    Green Arrow 2–6–2s, 161–2
    2–6–4Ts, 130

London & North Western Railway
    'Columbine', 20, 21
    'Cornwall', 24
    DX goods, 27–8
    Webb compounds, 44–7, 86
    Webb 2–4–0s, 43–5
    Precursors, 47, 48
    0–8–0s, 47, 76–7
London & South Western Railway
    Beattie 2–4–0Ts, 28–9
    Adams 4–4–2Ts, 62–4
    Adams 4–4–0s, 80, 81
    Adams 0–4–4Ts, 78, 79–80
    Drummond 4–2–2–0s, 86–7
    Drummond 4–4–0s, 93, 94
    Drummond 4–6–0s, 93
    Urie 4–6–0s, 131, 132
London Tilbury & Southend Railway
    4–4–2Ts, 58–60
Londonderry & Lough Swilly Railway
    8-coupled engines, 112–13

Metropolitan Railway
    Beyer, Peacock 4–4–0Ts, 30
    2–6–4Ts, 126, 130
Midland Railway
    Kirtley engines, 32–3
    Johnson single wheelers, 70–2
    Johnson 0–6–0Ts, 48, 50
    Johnson, Deeley & Fowler 0–6–0s, 51–53, 54
    Johnson & Deeley compounds, 99–102
    Paget 2–6–2, 113–14, 115
    0–10–0 banking engine, 133–4
Midland & Great Northern Joint Railway
    Johnson 0–6–0s, 51

North British Railway
    Holmes 0–6–0s, 72–3
    Atlantics, 92, 93
North Eastern Railway
    'Aerolite', 35–6
    Long boiler 0–6–0s, 26
    Fletcher 2–4–0s, 41

North Eastern Railway—*Contd.*
    Tennant 2–4–0s, 68
    Worsdell 4–4–0s, 80–1
    J72 class 0–6–0Ts, 88–9, 90
    0–8–0s, 77, 78

Padarn Railway
    'Fire Queen', 25

Shutt End Colliery
    'Agenoria', 15, 16
Snowdon Mountain Railway rack rail engines, 83–4
Somerset & Dorset Joint Railway
    0–6–0s, 51
    2–8–0s, 123, 124–5
South Eastern & Chatham Railway
    Wainwright engines, 96–8, 116, 117
    Maunsell engines, 125–8
Southern Railway
    Maunsell 'King Arthur' class, 131
    Maunsell 'Lord Nelson' class, 139, 140
    Maunsell 'Schools' class, 146–7
    Maunsell 2–6–0s, 127, 128
    Bulleid Q1 0–6–0s, 167–8
    Bulleid Pacifics, 163–7
    Bulleid Leaders, 174–6
Steam Tram engines, 64–5, 66
Stockton & Darlington Railway
    Locomotion No 1, 11, 12, 13
    'Derwent', 19, 22
    Long boiler engines, 26
Swindon Marlborough & Andover Railway
    0–4–4T, 57–8

Talyllyn Railway, 31

Vale of Rheidol Railway, 105–6
Vertical boiler engines, 56–7

Wantage Tramway
    'Shannon', 26–7
War Department
    0–6–0STs, 168–9

        2–8–0s, 169–70
        2–10–0s, 171
Welshpool & Llanfair Railway, 111
Wylam Colliery,
        'Wylam Dilly' (oldest steam locomotive still in
        existence), 10, 11